JADE: STONE OF HEAVEN

JADE:
STONE OF HEAVEN

By RICHARD GUMP

DOUBLEDAY & COMPANY, INC.

Garden City, New York

ISBN: 0-385-01705-7

LIBRARY OF CONGRESS CATALOG CARD NUMBER 62–12100

COPYRIGHT © 1962 BY RICHARD GUMP
15   14

. . . jade is a possession to be cherished by anyone who can find it or buy it or steal it. Chinese women ask for jade ornaments for their hair, and old men keep in their closed palms a piece of cool jade, so smooth that it seems soft to the touch. Rich men buy jades instead of putting their money in banks, for jade grows more beautiful with age. When men die, their families put jade in the tombs with them to keep them from decay and the orifices of their bodies are stopped with jade for purity. The poorest courtesan has her bit of jade to hang in her ears or to use in a hairpin, and the most successful and popular actresses wear jade instead of diamonds, because jade is the most sumptuous jewel against a woman's flesh . . .

PEARL S. BUCK
My Several Worlds

DYNASTIC CHART

CHINA

PREHISTORIC:

Painted Pottery Culture (YANG-SHAO) ⎱ ?–*c.* 2000
Black Pottery Culture (LUNG-SHAN) ⎰ or 1766 B.C.

DYNASTIES:

HSIA	(Legendary ?–*c.* 1766 B.C.)
SHANG	*c.* 1766 or 1550 B.C.–1122 or 1050 B.C.
CHOU	*c.* 1122 or 1050 B.C.–256 B.C.*
CH'IN	255–206 B.C.
HAN	206 B.C.–A.D. 220
THREE KINGDOMS	220–280
SIX DYNASTIES	280–589
SUI	589–618
T'ANG	618–907
FIVE DYNASTIES	907–960
SUNG	960–1279

(Northern Sung 960–1125)
(Southern Sung 1125–1279)

YÜAN	1260–1368
MING	1368–1644
CH'ING	1644–1912
REPUBLIC	1912–

*The earliest date on which the various chronologies agree is 841 B.C. All prior dates are tentative and vary from 150 to 200 years.

CONTENTS

Ground Away • Cool Jade • Scholars and Archers' Rings • III. TAOISM
AND JADE: FOOD FOR THE IMMORTALS • Tao: The Way • Food for the
Immortals • The Pure August Jade Emperor • The Eight Immortals
The Magic Elixir of Eternal Life • IV. BUDDHISM AND JADE • New
Dimensions for an Art • The Pagoda • Buddhas, Lohans, and Bo-
dhisattvas • Kuan Yin • Buddhist Symbols • Stone of an Enlarged Heaven
Zen • V. CHRISTIANITY, MOHAMMEDANISM, AND JADE • The Fateful
Decree • Monopoly Without Change

NEOLITHIC ERA • The Missing Years • Legendary or Historical? • SHANG
DYNASTY • A Fantastic Grandeur • CHOU DYNASTY • Girdle Jades • The
Message of Jade • The First Vessels • CH'IN DYNASTY • A Most Hated
Man • HAN DYNASTY • The Jade Coffin • Stylistic Affinities • THE THREE
KINGDOMS, SIX DYNASTIES, AND SUI DYNASTY • Transition • T'ANG DYNASTY
Yang Kuei-fei: China's Most Beautiful Woman • FIVE DYNASTIES AND SUNG
DYNASTY • Ritual Bronzes in Jade • YÜAN DYNASTY • Kublai and Genghis
Khan • MING DYNASTY • A New Vigor • Snuff Bottles • Musical Instru-
ments • CH'ING DYNASTY • K'ang Hsi • Ch'ien Lung • Aladdin's Dis-
covery • The Jade Dynasties: Conclusion and Continuation

I. BURMA'S JADE • The Discovery of Jadeite • Mining Burmese Jadeite
The Second Mystical Gift from Heaven • From Burma to China • The
World's Greatest Gamble • The Colors of Jadeite • A Debunking: The
Uses and Dating of Jadeite • The Graduated Bead Necklaces • II. PRE-
COLUMBIAN JADE • Jadeite and the Pre-Columbians • Montezuma, Cortés,
and Jade • Antiquity and Carving • Similarities in Pre-Columbian and
Chinese Uses of Jade • The Land Bridge • The Mysteries

Early Jade Carving • Jade's Technical Evolution • Water, Sand, and a
Piece of String • The Sword That Cuts Jade • Abrasives • Pao Yao:
The Mysterious Powder • FROM MOUNTAIN TO CARVING • Bidding for
Jade • What Does It Contain? • Sawing • Inking the Design • Roughing
It • Drilling, Gouging, and Grinding • Polishing • THE ANONYMOUS
ARTISTS • The Chinese Romeo and Juliet

CHAPTER NINE: MODERN JADE

FROM CH'IEN LUNG TO MAO TSE-TUNG • The Heritage of Ch'ien Lung
The Emperor's Seal • The Boxer Rebellion: End of an Era • THE WEST'S
DISCOVERY OF JADE • Looking West to the East • The Jade Room • The
Fall of the Ch'ing Dynasty • The Exposition • Jade Buying in China
The Comprador • Pigeons and Jade • Jade Hunting • The Ch'ien Lung
Jades • The Jade Rush • Liu's Jade • The Darkest Hours • Jade's
Victory

CHAPTER TEN: BUYING A "PIECE OF HEAVEN"

TRUE AND PSEUDO JADE • Is It Yü? The Price of a Single Word • Similar
to . . . • NOTABLE JADE FRAUDS • Dyed Jade Jewelry • Copies • BUYING
ANTIQUE JADE • What to Look For • Material • Workmanship • The
Feel of Jade • The Price of Jade • Are There Bargains in Jade? • Basic
Rules for Buying Jade • JADE: A CONCLUSION AND A BEGINNING . . .

COLOR ILLUSTRATIONS

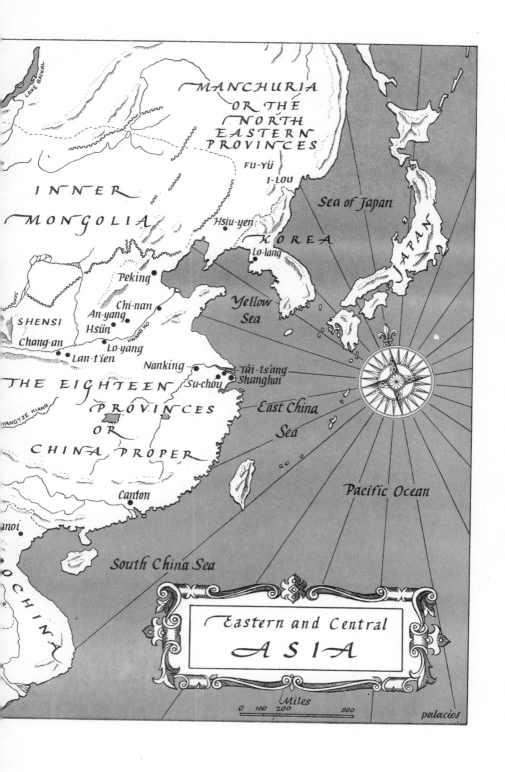

Eastern and Central ASIA

CHAPTER ONE

WHAT IS JADE?

If Jade is discarded and pearls destroyed, petty thieves will disappear, there being no valuables left to steal.

From a dictionary published during the reign of the
Emperor K'ang Hsi (A.D. 1662–1722)

Han Dynasty horse's head. Similar to the pottery horses of
the same period. Carved in the round, of deep green nephrite.
H: 8½″. L: 5¼″. Courtesy Fogg Art Museum, Harvard University, Cambridge, Massachusetts. Grenville L. Winthrop
collection.

Jade is no ordinary stone.

Not even an ordinary "precious" stone.

It has a "certain something" that made a Chinese emperor offer fifteen cities for a jade carving he could hold in one hand; that made Montezuma smile when he heard that Cortés was interested only in gold, since Montezuma's most precious possession was jade. That caused men of civilizations oceans and centuries apart to believe it to be the stone of immortality. That made some men forbid it to their wives, and other men speak through it to their gods, and still others spend years carving a single object from it.

For there is a magic about jade that seems to elude man's definition, that sets it apart from all other stones. A mystery that lies beyond man's appreciation of its rarity or the skillful carving of its surface; that entices and comes closest to revealing itself when man handles "the stone of Heaven." A special, hidden beauty that causes men, when they speak of jade, to speak in the language of myth and legend—ordinary words are limited; the special quality within the jade stone is not.

"An inherent poetry without words," one Chinese author called it. "A window to reality," wrote another. "Better a broken piece of jade than a whole tile" is one Chinese proverb. "In plenteous years, jade, in years of drought, grain, is what is needed," states another.

The Central Asians placed a huge slab of jade before the tomb of Tamerlane to make it inviolate. The pre-Columbians made sacrificial knives from it. Aladdin expressed wonder at the fabulous trees of jade in the underground cavern. The Russians carved a whole sarcophagus, for Czar Alexander III, of jade. In both New Zealand and New Caledonia a jade *mere* or war club was the chief's symbol of authority. Fathers in the Loyalty Islands once bartered their daughters for jade. China built a civilization around the stone.

What is this "magic" that makes jade the stone of superlatives, the quintessence of creation, a gift from Heaven?

We catch glimpses of the answer as we unravel the geological and cultural history of jade. For some men not only sensed this special other-worldly quality, they came close to capturing it, in myth, poetry, or, more graphically, in carving.

Aladdin expressed wonder at the fabulous trees . . . Jade trees, the bowls, leaves, and fruitage composed of varicolored pieces of nephrite and jadeite. H: app. 22″. 20th century. Formerly in the author's collection.

More Precious Than Gold

The American girl dreams of a gold band, preferably ornamented with diamonds. Our monetary standard is based on gold. But to the Chinese, earth's most precious treasure is neither gold nor diamonds. The Chinese maiden dreams of *jade*.

In contests of skill in ancient China the ivory scepter was awarded to the man who came in third, the gold scepter to the man who placed second. The victor received the scepter of jade.

The same order held true in courtly attire. Only royalty of the first rank was permitted the ceremonial use of the finest jade.

An ancient Chinese legend tells us that even within the earth

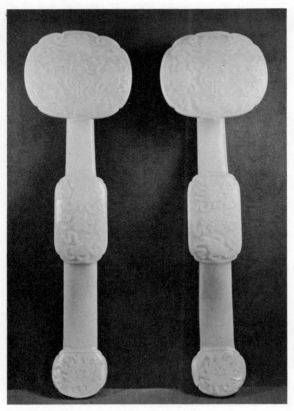

The victor received the scepter of jade . . . The *Ju-I*, or scepter. Pure-white nephrite. L: 17″. 18th century. Courtesy M. H. De Young Memorial Museum, San Francisco, California. Avery Brundage collection.

jade and gold are worlds apart, that they repel each other, since gold is of the material realm and jade is of the spirit.

We need not travel so far back to witness the distinction. We can find it in one of the folk tales of the American West.

In the late 1870s the gold rush was over in California, the gold fields deserted except for a few dogged old prospectors who had little more than belief and memory to go on. Luck was with some of these men, however; occasionally there would be rumors of a new "find," supported by fistfuls of the yellow mineral.

But it was a strange kind of luck. The gold was found not in new veins but on claims that showed every sign of having already been worked.

Slowly a curious picture took shape. Many of these claims had been staked and mined by venerable gentlemen from the Celestial Kingdom. Yet while Caucasians around them went mad with gold fever, the Chinese quietly took from the earth not the less worthy gold, but raw jade, which they shipped back to the land of their ancestors, where it was appreciated. The gold, *it is said*, they left in the ground, untouched.

Apocryphal? Probably. But no more unbelievable than many of the "documented" Chinese accounts regarding jade.

If it *really* happened, these Chinese showed great wisdom and foresight, as gold can be mined in many places today, while jade is known to exist in only a few locations, with both quality and quantity diminishing.

One suspects that had the vision of these men extended to the present they would have laughed, since there would come a time when Americans would spend considerable sums, backed by gold, to buy single pieces of jade; when some of the finest jade carvings would rest in the private collections and museums of America and Europe.

I think they might have been too astonished to laugh had they foreseen that the descendants of their grimy, bearded neighbors would one day also appreciate the aesthetics of jade, even get the "feel" of its potent mystery.

What Is Jade?

Many would answer: "A green stone that comes from China."

They would be wrong on three counts.

First, jade comes in every shade of the rainbow (plus a few, according to the Chinese, that mortal man cannot see). Even in the accustomed *green* there are dozens of distinct hues, bearing such colorful names as kingfisher, spinach, emerald, moss, and young onion green.

Second, *jade is not one stone but two: the minerals nephrite and jadeite,* each with its distinctive characteristics, properties, colors, sources, and uses. Though the differences between the two are highly significant, too few writers have, for one reason or another, bothered to distinguish clearly between them.

Nephrite is a silicate of magnesium—fibrous, hard to fracture, almost soapy in appearance. Jadeite is a silicate of aluminum,

Jade is not one stone, but two: nephrite, the older stone, fibrous, hard to fracture, almost soapy in appearance . . . Mountain scene, carved from a pebble of dark green nephrite from Chinese Turkestan. H: 8½". w: 6". 18th century or earlier. Courtesy M. H. De Young Memorial Museum, San Francisco, California. Avery Brundage collection.

. . . and jadeite, the young stone, microcrystalline, much more readily broken, and when polished far more brilliant . . . Lotus bowl of light green Burmese jadeite. H: 8". w: 6". 20th century. Courtesy M. H. De Young Memorial Museum, San Francisco, California. Avery Brundage collection.

microcrystalline, much more readily broken, and, when polished, far more brilliant.

Jadeite is a comparatively young stone, in terms of carving, having been used in China to any great extent only since 1784. Small wonder, then, that some dealers do not bother to make a clear distinction between the two stones, inasmuch as *most* of the "ancient" jadeite pieces on their shelves are considerably less than one hundred years old.

The jade we know as nephrite is as old as China's recorded history, a part of its first myths and legends. We may be sure that the piece of jade which tradition tells us was carried by a unicorn to the mother of Confucius, announcing his impending birth with the inscription "the son of the essence of water shall succeed to the withering China and be a throneless king," was nephrite, not jadeite. Confucius, who lived six hundred years before Christ and was one of the world's most eloquent spokesmen for jade, never saw the bright green stone which is today commonly associated with the word. For Confucius never knew the beautiful gem jade, which is jadeite.

Third, though the use of jade is inseparably linked with the development of Chinese worship, court ceremonials, thought, and art, we have no evidence that jade (of either variety) was ever found in the earth of China itself. We believe it was mined there thousands of years ago and, as elsewhere in the world, the supply was in time exhausted, but we have no proof. So the stone which determined, directed, and changed the course of Chinese history is, in so far as positive evidence goes, an import.

The Semantics of Jade

What image does the name *jade* conjure up for you?

A kidney stone? Alas, that is the original meaning of the word.

The Chinese word for it was *yü*. The pictograph for this word (王) is said to have originated in 2950 B.C., five thousand years ago, when the transition from knotted cords to written signs supposedly occurred. It represents three pieces of jade (三) pierced and threaded with a string (|). The dot was added to distinguish it from the pictograph for "ruler." (Common to ruler and jade was the function of serving as intermediary between earth and Heaven.) And though at times writers used *yü* to describe numerous carved stones (it was sometimes used as indiscriminately as our word

Ironically, the stone found in Central and South America and Mexico was not nephrite at all . . . Pre-Columbian plaque of cream-colored jadeite. Zapotec period. Courtesy National Gallery of Art, Washington, D.C. Robert Woods Bliss collection.

golden), it generally meant "a precious stone of great beauty." But it was not the Chinese who gave us the word *jade*.

Early Spanish navigators brought from Mexico a curious green stone known, because of its purported medicinal properties, as *piedra de ijada*, "stone of the flank or of the loins," and *piedra de los riñones*, "stone of the kidneys," the belief being that if one wore it next to the skin it would cure kidney trouble. In 1595

Sir Walter Raleigh wrote of it, mentioning its use "for spleen stones."

Translated into French, this should have become *pierre de l'ejade,* but through a printer's error it was rendered *le jade.* The brevity-minded English quickly simplified it to *jade.*

Piedra de los riñones went through its own transformation. In Latin it was called *lapis nephriticus, nephros* being the Greek word for kidney. Thus came the word *nephrite,* which was somewhat ironic, since much later it was discovered that the stone found in Central and South America and Mexico was not nephrite at all but jadeite.

The word *jadeite* is a comparative newcomer. The French scientist Damour coined it in 1863 to distinguish between the emerald-green stone of Burma and the nephrite of remote Turkestan.

The horses are always spirited and fresh . . . Horse. White nephrite with light greenish tint. H: 6". L: 8⅓". W: 3". Possibly Ming Dynasty. Courtesy Metropolitan Museum of Art, New York. Heber R. Bishop collection.

. . . the women are never disreputable . . . Lady. Gray nephrite. H: 6¾″.
Han Dynasty. Courtesy Chicago Natural History Museum, Chicago, Illinois.

Totally unrelated is the word *jade*, which means "a tired horse" or "a disreputable woman," and *jaded*, meaning "exhausted" or "worn out." The horses we encounter in jade carvings are nearly always spirited and fresh; the women, more spirit than flesh, are certainly never disreputable, though the women in some of the Chinese tales concerning the stone are another matter.

Confucius and the Scientists

But we still haven't answered the question: *What is jade?*

Nearly twenty-four hundred years ago Confucius stated that if jade is highly valued it is because, *since ancient times,*

the wise have likened it to virtue. For them, its polish and brilliancy represent the whole of purity; its perfect compactness and extreme hardness represent the sureness of the intelligence; its angles, which do not cut, although they seem sharp, represent justice; the pure and prolonged sound which it gives forth when one strikes it represents music.

Its color represents loyalty; its interior flaws, always showing themselves through the transparency, call to mind sincerity; its iridescent brightness represents heaven; its admirable substance, born of mountain

Its angles, which do not cut, although they seem sharp, represent justice . . . Lidded vase. Sea-green nephrite with specks of brown. H: 8½". W: 5¾". 18th or 19th century. Courtesy M. H. De Young Memorial Museum, San Francisco, California. Avery Brundage collection.

and of water, represents the earth. Used alone without ornamentation it represents chastity. The price which all the world attaches to it represents the truth. To support these comparisons, the Book of Verse says: "When I think of a wise man, his merits appear to be like jade." And that is why the wise set so great store by jade . . .

It is curious that while in many fields science has supplanted legend, in the story of jade, myth and reality often meet comfortably. As early as the sixth century B.C. we find Confucius discovering parallels to the highest human virtues in the actual mineral structure of the stone. It remains only for science to be more explicit.

". . . its perfect compactness and extreme hardness . . ."

Smash two diamonds together and one will break. Bring two pieces of nephrite together with all the force you can muster, and the result will be only a loud sound; the stones will remain intact.

Nephrite is the world's *toughest* stone.

Nephrite's unusual toughness is due to its fibrous texture. For an idea of this toughness: in one test a weight of fifty tons was required to crush one cubic inch of nephrite. Jadeite, being granulated, fractures a little more easily.

Its iridescent brightness represents heaven . . . Bowl with ring handles. Gray-green and white nephrite. H: 2½". D: 9½". 18th century. Courtesy M. H. De Young Memorial Museum, San Francisco, California. Avery Brundage collection.

Diamond, corundum, and topaz are *harder* than the two varieties of jade. This means, on the Moh's scale for hardness, that these three will scratch jade. But jade in turn will scratch granite, apatite, fluorite, marble, gypsum, and talc. By this standard, nephrite is rated approximately 6.5, jadeite 6.75, too close to make this an accurate scale for distinguishing between them, but useful in separating both from their imitators. To distinguish between the two, a gravity test is often used; the gravity of nephrite is 3.00, while that of jadeite is 3.32.

Nephrite's fibrous nature makes it a great challenge to the craftsman. Yet, as overcompensation, its toughness makes possible the rendering of plates, bowls, and vases paper-thin, as well as the cutting of chains from solid blocks of stone. Nephrite is the better material, in general, for such elaborate work, but the superb craftsmen of China have successfully wrought the more sensitive jadeite in similar fashion.

People marvel—"Think of it, he carved this out of hardwood" —when the real marvel would be had he carved a well-defined piece out of soft pine. It is the same with jade and soapstone. It is easy to cut soapstone. A little pressure and the tool cuts right through it, therefore making it difficult to obtain a fine carving. While jade, which often takes months of patient labor to cut, by its very strength makes possible unusually subtle and exact carving.

". . . its polish and brilliancy represent the whole of purity . . ."

Pure jade is white jade. Color comes from the presence of other minerals in the stone. The smooth, soft, glossy appearance that the world identifies with jade is the result of the application of the mysterious polishing abrasive, *pao yao*, to the tough surface of the stone. Jadeite, being crystalline, takes the higher polish and possesses a greater brilliance. Both nephrite and jadeite are often translucent and, in very rare instances, transparent.

". . . its angles, which do not cut, although they seem sharp . . ."

Confucius was, of course, speaking of nephrite, whose fibrous structure gives a wavy, hard-soft texture to the surface, apparent under high magnification. With the use of slow abrasives this gives even to the edges of a carving a pleasing softness.

". . . its iridescent brightness represents heaven; its admirable substance, born of mountain and of water, represents the earth. Used alone without ornamentation it represents chastity. The price

Its very strength makes possible unusually subtle and exact carving . . . Pair of vases. The body, chain, and lid of each was carved from a single piece of light green nephrite, an excellent example of 20th-century carving. H: 7". W: 3". Courtesy M. H. De Young Memorial Museum, San Francisco, California. Avery Brundage collection.

which all the world attaches to it represents the truth . . . 'When I think of a wise man, his merits appear to be like jade' . . ."

Here we encounter a problem; we reach the limits of science. For even after we have deciphered the chemical composition of jade and unfolded the many fables and facts which surround it, we have left, undiminished, the fantastic beauty and magic of the stone itself.

What is there about jade that brings out the highest in man—the sublime skill of an anonymous artist, the innately simple yet profound truths that one may realize upon getting "the feel of jade?" Why has the stone played such an important part in Chinese history, religion, literature, thought, and art? Why is it, to quote one writer, "the most completely Chinese of all materials, though much of it was imported from other countries?" Why has it received, to quote another, "the most fanatical and revered adulation ever bestowed by man upon any of nature's gifts?" Why is it credited with so many mystical powers, such as safeguarding health, assuring happiness, preventing decay of the body? Why do the Chinese consider it their most sacred gift, believing that in giving jade they are giving a part of themselves? What is the strange affinity of women and jade that the Chinese would send young virgins to wade naked in streams at night to attract it? What makes jade so precious that present-day Chinese would dig up the graves of their ancestors to find it? What is its potent power that even the Chinese Communists could not succeed for long in suppressing it?

Within the stone itself is a complete world that draws from man his highest aspirations, his noblest dreams, and his greatest creativity. To enter and explore this realm we must go back in time, before the beginning of the earth, to discover why nephrite became known as *the stone of Heaven.*

CHAPTER TWO

NEPHRITE: STONE OF HEAVEN, EARTH, AND MAN

The spirit of jade is called Wei Fan and is said to resemble a beautiful woman. If anyone desires to meet her, he must clothe himself in blue raiment, and calling her by name thrust with a reed-blade, then she will appear. If anyone going out into the night espies a woman carrying a candle, who vanishes into a stone, then will jade be found in that stone.

Chinese folklore
Pai tse tu

Dancer. Two views. Translucent white nephrite. H: 3¾". Chou Dynasty. Courtesy Freer Gallery of Art, Washington, D.C.

I. THE STONE OF HEAVEN

The First Carver

Long before the creation of the earth, before mountain rivers ran and men spoke and the valleys echoed with thunder, jade existed, according to one Chinese legend.

In the beginning, say the Chinese Taoists, there was a great Void, in which was created Chaos, which in time differentiated into Light and Dark. The Dark was called Yin; it was negative, female, its symbol the moon, or sometimes the earth, since its force was centripetal, downward-pulling. The Light was called Yang; it was male, positive, represented by the sun, its force centrifugal, outgoing, the spirit's flight.

Pan Ku, the first carver,
creating the universe.

The two principles met, merged briefly, and from this union the god Pan Ku was formed.

At first it did not appear to be a very impressive mating. For Pan Ku was a dwarf—but a dwarf with a mission. With his two hands, a hammer, and a chisel, he immediately set about carving the universe out of Chaos.

Four supernatural beings appeared to help this first carver: the Unicorn, the Tortoise, the Phoenix, and the Dragon. Whence they came, no one knows. We do know that the latter pair were regarded as the essence of Yang, the male principle, and were said to be composed of white and azure jade.

As Pan Ku labored, his stature increased—in proportion to his accomplishments. Each day he worked he grew six feet, and he carved for eighteen thousand years. When he died he was so large, and so engrossed in his task, that he became a part of his creation.

His flesh became the soil of the earth, his limbs its four quarters, his head the mountains. His veins were now rivers, his skin plants, his hair trees, his teeth and bones minerals, his marrow precious stones. His right eye gave light to the sun, his left to the moon. His sweat fell as rain. And his last breath became thunder, clouds, and wind. The wind impregnated the parasites that fed on his body, and the result was Man.

The Storm God took pity . . . Flat ax. Ivory-colored nephrite. L: 4¾″. w: 3½″. T: ¼″. Shang Dynasty. Courtesy Art Institute of Chicago, Chicago, Illinois. Edward and Louise B. Sonnenschein collection.

Forged from the Rainbow: The Stone of Heaven

Another legend, of even greater antiquity, is more explicit concerning the origin of jade and somewhat less belittling of man. This time we find man already stumbling helplessly about the earth, the prey of all the wild animals. But the Storm God, looking down from the heavens, takes pity. With one hand he grasps the rainbow and with the other he forges it into jade axes. These he throws down for man to find.

Man, eventually discovering them, guesses the origin of his precious gift and thereafter calls jade *the stone of Heaven.*

Dragon Tears

A third legend, which obviously originated much later than the preceding two, states that when China was invaded by the Tartar barbarians, the Imperial Dragon shed tears of sorrow, and these tears petrified into jade.

II. THE STONE OF EARTH

The Origin of Jade

As these legends indicate, the ancient Chinese considered jade no ordinary stone. Geologists and mineralogists agree. They tell us that once the earth was a seething, gaseous mass like our sun, and perhaps part of it. When this mass started to cool there was great turbulence, odd pressures, strange fusions. Some minerals and rock mixtures were commonplace; others, like diamonds, were rarities occurring in only a few locations. Both varieties of jade are among the uncommon minerals. Jadeite (a pyroxene) is formed twenty to thirty miles below the surface of the earth, under tremendous heat and pressure, and only through violent upheavals and erosion is it brought up to the light. Nephrite (an amphibole), though similar in many ways to jadeite, is formed closer to the earth's surface, through the interaction of calcium, magnesium, and water. Or, as the Chinese put it, it is "the essence of hill and stream."

When scientists say jade is fortuitous and the Chinese that it was a gift from Heaven, they agree in all except terminology.

River and Mountain Jade: The Sources of Nephrite

If the jade thrown down from Heaven by the Storm God was embedded in the soil of China itself, it was depleted by the time

China's recorded history began. To date we have no evidence—only a strong supposition—that China ever mined the stone within its own provinces. The belief that jade and the art of carving it were brought to China by an earlier nomadic people has some adherents. S. Howard Hansford, one of the greatest jade authorities today, suggests that if an ancient people did carry the first jade into China "it may, indeed, have been the possession of these stone implements of superior toughness and keenness that gave the invaders victory over a ruder stone-age people already settled in the Yellow River basin."

Probably the earliest Chinese reference to the source of jade occurs in the writing of Huai-nan Tzŭ, philosopher of the House of Han (*c.* 200 B.C.), who mentions that *yü* from Chung San (later identified as the K'un Lun Mountains) was heated in a furnace for three days and nights without change in its color, polish, or texture.

The *Shih chi*, a history from the second century B.C. and the *Ch'ien Han shu*, of about the same date, both identify Khotan in Central Asia as a source of jade.

For more than two thousand years the chief source of China's nephrite has been the Khotan-Yarkand area in what is now Chinese Turkestan.

Khotan is located on an oasis in the Taklamakan Desert, surrounded on three sides by shifting sand and on the fourth by the wild K'un Lun Mountains. From high in this remote range two rivers, the Black Jade River (Kara-kāsh) and the White Jade River (Yurung-kāsh), flow down through Khotan, carrying in their descent the precious pebbles and boulders so valuable to far-off Cathay.

The possession of these implements of superior toughness and keenness may have meant victory over a ruder stone-age people . . . Dagger-ax. Green-yellow nephrite. L: 17⅝". W: 4⅜". Shang Dynasty. Courtesy Freer Gallery of Art, Washington, D.C.

Khotan lies also on one of the world's great trade routes and for over two thousand years has sent jade-bearing caravans into China, either as tribute (when Khotan was a dependency of the empire) or as trade. Only wars and national hostilities have interrupted, for brief periods, this long-standing commerce.

Nephrite is believed to have been found first in the rivers and streams of Turkestan, in the form of pebbles and boulders, and later mined, when its sources were discovered upriver in the K'un Lun Mountains.

Marco Polo

In 1272, Marco Polo, passing through this area, noted in his *Travels* that large numbers of "chalcedonies and jaspers" were found in the streams and when transported to Cathay "fetched great

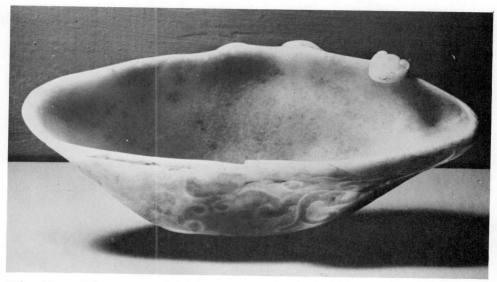

What Marco Polo saw was probably jade . . . Wine cup in the form of a rhinoceros horn, decorated with low-relief dragons in the style of the late Chou Dynasty, with a high-relief dragon peering over the rim. Rhinoceros horn cups were supposed to detect poison. White nephrite with brownish-yellow markings. L: 6½″. H: 2¼″. Sung Dynasty. Courtesy Walker Art Center, Minneapolis, Minnesota. T. B. Walker collection.

Plate 1 It is not age, but the quality of the stone and the skill of the carver that determine the worth of a jade carving. These spirited jadeite horses were carved during the 20th century. H: 6″. L: 8¼″. Author's collection.

prices." Most scholars believe what he really saw was nephrite. It is known that upon his return to Venice, when he emptied his pockets of his treasures and was only then "recognized" by his relatives, there was no jade among his possessions. This is not surprising, since jade (or jasper or chalcedonies) then had no value in the West, and Marco Polo was primarily a merchant. Besides, much of the carved jade he might have seen in China would have been too bulky to carry, even had he admired it. This was five hundred years before the discovery of the Imperial jewel jade (jadeite), which he certainly wouldn't have overlooked.

The Disguised Priest and the Mines

A more detailed viewing of this area and jade hunting, as seen through Western eyes, occurred when the Jesuit astronomer Benedict Göes visited Khotan and Yarkand in 1603. Called to Peking to help revise the Chinese calendar, Göes traveled in the disguise of a levantine merchant to avoid persecution as a Christian. Although he died before reaching his intended destination, he spent eleven months in the Yarkand and wrote at length on jade and the mining of it.

After mentioning the great value set upon jade by the Chinese and its importance in trading, Göes noted:

> There are two kinds of it; the first and more valuable is got out of the river Cotan [Khotan], not far from the capital, almost in the same way that divers fish for gems, and this is usually extracted in pieces about as big as large flints. The other and inferior kind is excavated from the mountains; the larger masses are split into slabs some two ells [éll=app. 7 feet] broad and then these are reduced to a size adapted for carriage [in other words to a camel load]. That mountain is some twenty days journey from this capital . . .
>
> The extraction of these blocks is a work involving immense labour owing to the hardness of the substance as well as to the remote and lonely position of the place. They say that the stone is sometimes softened by the application of a blazing fire on the surface. The right of quarrying here is also sold by the King at a high price to some merchant, without whose licence no other speculators can dig there during the term of the lease. When a party of workmen goes thither they take a year's provisions along with them, for they do not usually revisit the populated districts at a shorter interval.

This was neither Göes's first nor last contact with jade—on one occasion it saved his life.

The Princess repaid him with the most precious substance known to her . . .
Lion medallion. White nephrite with light grayish tint. H: 2¾″. W: 2⅓″. T: ⅓″.
Ming Dynasty. Courtesy Metropolitan Museum of Art, New York. Heber R.
Bishop collection.

While en route to Yarkand he had encountered the sister of the
King of Kashgar. On her way to Mecca the Princess had run short
of funds and had appealed to the merchants for loans, which she
promised to repay with ample interest. Göes lent her six hundred
pieces of gold, refusing to take her bond. When they reached
Yarkand she repaid him in jade, the most precious substance known
to her, and in an amount far surpassing her debt. After leaving
Yarkand, Göes journeyed to Suchow, a Moslem community with
little use for Christians. Since Göes preached everywhere he went,
his merchant's disguise was not very effective. He was delayed

here and was charged exorbitant prices for food and lodging, in hopes of bringing him to starvation. When all his other resources were gone he finally sold the Princess's jade, thereby gaining sufficient revenue to pay his large debts and still have funds for another year.

Moonlight and Naked Maidens

Despite the erroneous assumption that the fire softened the stone (it cracked it), Göes's observations are far more accurate than those of the *T'ien kung k'ai wu*, a compendium of crafts and industries published some thirty years later, in 1637. On the origin of jade, this Chinese reference work says:

"Jade is embedded in the rocky structure of the mountain. Before the torrent has dislodged it, the jade in the mass is soft, like cotton fibre; after being dislodged it hardens and once it is exposed to the air it becomes still harder."

On the mining of river jade, this work of Sung Ying-hsing is only slightly less fanciful:

> The jade in its natural state does not lie deep below the surface of the earth, and the stream descending in a wild torrent causes it to emerge. Those who collect it, however, do not take it at the place where it first appears, since the force of the current would prevent their working there. When the river is full in summer months, the jade follows the current down for one, two, or three hundred *li* [*li*=⅓ mile], when it can be taken from the river. Jade reflects moonlight. So when the native jade-hunters of the river regions search the rivers on moonlight nights in autumn, as they mostly do, they scrutinize those places where the jade collects for an intensified glow of the quality of moonlight. The jade is carried down with the flow, but mingled with all kinds of different stones, and only after they have been fetched out of the shallow streams and examined, are the results known.

Nephrite, as found in the rivers, is thickly coated with an oxidized "skin" or "rind," which must be ground down before the jade itself can be seen. It is very hard to distinguish from an ordinary boulder, although jade-hunting families in Turkestan claim to have a secret method for detecting it, which they reveal only to their eldest sons. Though the stone does not lack miraculous properties, it is unlikely that reflecting moonlight off this hard dark "skin" is among them.

Plate 2 Ming vase of the variety known as "chicken bone," from Chinese Turkestan. H, with cover: 8¼". Author's collection.

The account gets more fantastic, though not less interesting, as it progresses. It states that it was the custom in the region to make young maidens strip and walk naked in the streams at night. Being female (*yin*) they would attract the male (*yang*) jade. Feeling it nuzzling against their feet, they would then reach down and land it.

A later account, less bare but more reputable, notes that hired men hunted the stone in the rivers and streams by day, each hunter stooping to pick up any pebble resembling jade as he saw it. A scribe on the bank would strike a gong, then mark down each worker's stoops alongside his name in a big ledger. At the end of the allotted time the hunter would have to produce from his apron the same number of stones.

Mining Mountain Jade

Mountain jade was mined much as Göes described it, and is even to the present day, in both the Yarkand and Khotan regions. Jade hunters would travel high into "the remote and lonely" mountainous region in West Chinese Turkestan. After locating the outcroppings of nephrite, one of two methods of mining would be utilized.

The older method was to build charcoal fires near the vein; at night, when the temperature changed, the stone would crack. In the morning the workmen would drive wooden wedges into the cracks to break off the stone. The other technique was to drill holes and fill them with water; with the arrival of winter, the water would freeze and crack the stone. In spring the hunters would return, rolling the blocks of jade down to the valleys below, where they would be loaded on camelback to begin the arduous two-thousand-mile journey to Peking. Of course much fine jade was lost by both methods. Lost, too, were a number of caravans, which, molested by robbers, never reached the Chinese capital.

These camel caravans are mentioned frequently by travelers throughout the eighteenth century and in even more recent times, for the Jade Route is still used today.

The jade taken from Turkestan varied from pebble size to mammoth blocks weighing several tons. During the reign of the Emperor Ch'ien Lung (1736–95), which is today famous for its artistic production, four exceptionally large blocks of nephrite were carved in the Imperial workshops; the largest, over seven feet high, weighed nearly seven tons.

China's chief source of nephrite has shifted back and forth from Khotan to Yarkand since at least 200 B.C. But in recent years the material from these areas has been of consistently poor quality, indicating that these deposits, like most of the others in the world, have almost been worked out.

Other Sources

Other sources of nephrite have been Lake Baikal, in eastern Siberia; the South Island of New Zealand (where jade is called "greenstone"); Jordanow Slaski, Poland; the Frazer River Valley in British Columbia; Kotzebue in Alaska; and two sites in the United States. Of the above, New Zealand no longer permits export of the raw stone, several sites have been exhausted, and the remainder produce nephrite in such negligible quantities that the supply falls far short of the great demand.

"Spinach jade," distinguishable by the small flecks of black graphite embedded in the dark green stone . . . Censer with cover. H: 7¾". W: 4". 18th or 19th century. Courtesy M. H. De Young Memorial Museum, San Francisco, California. Avery Brundage collection.

Siberian Nephrite

Siberian nephrite is usually distinguishable from other varieties by the presence of small black flecks of graphite embedded in the stone, which is at its best a dark green. The Chinese call it "spinach jade," and it was from this material that in 1897 the sarcophagus of Czar Alexander III was carved.

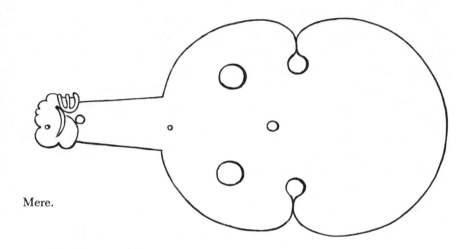

Mere.

New Zealand Greenstone

The Maoris of New Zealand—to whom metal was unknown until the arrival of Captain James Cook in 1769—prized nephrite above all other stones. They called it *pounamu* or "greenstone," and from it they carved axes, chisels, adzes, knives, jewelry, and the *mere* (pronounced meý-rey). The *mere* was the war club of their chieftain, which symbolized his authority and his title to the land. It was from thirteen to fifteen inches long, of flattened shape, with a hole drilled in the handle for the thong which fastened the club to the wrist. It was usually carved from stone especially chosen for its fine color and distinctive markings.

The Maoris, too, were not without their jade superstition. They would not let their women approach the jade cutters, though whether they were afraid of the effect of the females on the jade or the male stone upon the females is unknown. During pregnancy the women wore necklaces (*hei-tiki*) of jade which showed the embryo as it evolved into human form.

Jade in North America

In 1883, Lieutenant George M. Stoney of the U. S. Navy discovered that the Eskimos on the Arctic coast of Alaska were using jade tools. Accompanied by Eskimo guides, he traveled 150 miles up the Kobuk River to find the fabled Jade Mountain, the stone's reputed source, and to become probably the first jade explorer in North America.

The first time he failed to reach his destination; on the second trip he reached it, but the Eskimos refused to set foot on the mountain because they held it sacred. Stoney climbed it, accompanied by several other seamen, and joyfully brought down his find. The Smithsonian Institution pronounced it serpentine (a stone that looks like nephrite but is much softer, 2½ to 4 in hardness, compared to 6½, and much more readily fractured).

Undaunted, he made a third trip the following year and found nephrite "in place" on the mountain. It was an important discovery historically, but this site, like most others, soon exhausted its best material.

Wyoming Nephrite

The most important nephrite discovery in the United States occurred as late as 1942, near Lander, Wyoming. Of remarkably even texture and quality, free from flaws, fractures, and irregularities, the best of this nephrite was not long available. As might be expected, a Chinese-American, John Wenti Chang, quickly purchased several tons of the finest of this Wyoming stone. To all appearances, this site, too, has now surrendered its highest-quality nephrite.

The California Jade Rush

Jade has been found on the beaches of California from Crescent City in the north to San Diego in the south, usually in the form of pebbles, sometimes as boulders. The much-heralded jade rush of 1950, which centered mainly on the coastal region around Monterey, gave much pleasure to rockhounds but yielded little jade fit for carving. Nor have the several sources of nephrite and jadeite found elsewhere in California proved profitable. The nephrite found in large quantities in San Benito County, in common with much of the nephrite of British Columbia, is so heavily flawed as to render it unfit for use.

Plate 3 Maori Hei-tiki,
from New Zealand. H: 1″.
Courtesy M. H.
De Young Memorial
Museum, San Francisco,
California. Avery
Brundage collection.

Plate 4 Water buffaloes, carved from Wyoming nephrite. H: 2½″. L: 5½″.
20th century. Author's collection.

Wanted: A Jade Mountain

Today there is no single source producing the uniformly fine-quality nephrite once found in Chinese Turkestan. The price of both raw and carved jade all too clearly reflects this fact. Each year as the supply decreases, the demand, and hence the price, increases. There have been geological reports of nephrite findings in Brazil and in the Ligurian Apennines of Italy, but to date neither site has been explored sufficiently to determine the quality and quantity of the stone.

The world needs a Jade Mountain. Perhaps someday one will be found. Or maybe one day, as some believe, the "lost jade mines of China" will be rediscovered. Until then, and probably long after, fine jade will remain one of the earth's rarest and most coveted possessions.

III. THE STONE OF MAN

Man Meets Jade

Going back to that first man and his discovery of jade—assuming for a moment that we can give credence to the Chinese legend—one wonders why he would proclaim it the "stone of Heaven."

Let's dramatize that fateful meeting. . . .

From the bushes came a crash and a roar, and almost before he knew what was happening the great beast was upon him. He had time only to raise his club and swing once before being thrown back by the impact.

Cautiously, wondrously, he got back on his feet. He did not believe it; the other hunters back at the fire wouldn't believe it either—except the proof was before him. The great beast was dead. The animal's huge head had caved in as if it were a hollow gourd.

The hunter examined his club with an almost reverent wonder. The stone was still as firm and sound as when he had chanced upon it in the bed of a nearby stream. It was remarkable; unlike any stone he had known, it shattered everything he hit with it, including his older stone weapons.

What was this miraculous new substance?

Though the sky was growing dark and the beast had led him far from camp, he knelt down, placed his club on the ground before him, and gave thanks to the gods of nature for his hunting. Surely, this stone was a gift of Heaven. . . .

This is probably just about what happened.

A man found a stone so tough as to resist all efforts to break it, a stone that would neither chip nor flake, yet took and kept a good edge. Its toughness made it a superior weapon, and such a weapon meant survival. It is not surprising that he thought it to be a divine gift, nor that among the earliest jades to which we can assign conjectural dates are axheads, knives, and celts so small or so thin and delicately carved that we must surmise they were not real weapons but tokens used in ritual and religious ceremonials, perhaps long after their original meaning and use had been forgotten.

Toughness made it a superior weapon, and such a weapon meant survival . . . Dagger-ax. Mottled green nephrite. L: 11½". W: 4¼". T: ¼". Courtesy Art Institute of Chicago, Chicago, Illinois. Edward and Louise B. Sonnenschein collection.

Earliest Uses

Lacking tangible evidence, we can only guess how jade was used before it assumed ritual form and was placed in tombs. We know, however, that in all early civilizations primitive man survived by using the toughest substances available to him. Toughness made a stone an ideal weapon for defense against beasts and other men; it also—perhaps equally important in the long run—could be fashioned into a tool sufficiently strong to harness the forces of nature. Perhaps, like flint and other counterparts in Western civilization,

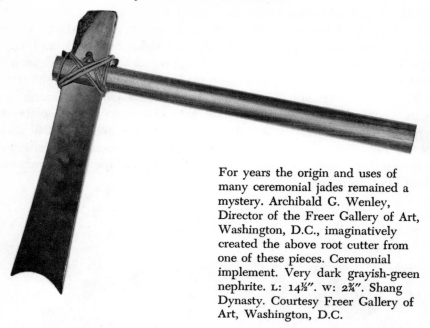

For years the origin and uses of
many ceremonial jades remained a
mystery. Archibald G. Wenley,
Director of the Freer Gallery of Art,
Washington, D.C., imaginatively
created the above root cutter from
one of these pieces. Ceremonial
implement. Very dark grayish-green
nephrite. L: 14½". w: 2¾". Shang
Dynasty. Courtesy Freer Gallery of
Art, Washington, D.C.

jade was once used to till the soil, to dig channels to guide streams,
and to break less sturdy stones for building purposes.

With these uses would come, almost simultaneously, respect for
the qualities of the stone. Toughness=Survival=Life=Worship may
well be the equation which explains why, of all stones, jade has
had the longest unbroken connection with religious usage.

A Jade Age

With the discovery of bits of worked stone or metal, scientists
have been able to plot the course of civilization through different
eras: the eolithic, in which man used implements of rough bone
or naturally formed chipped flints; the paleolithic, in which man
himself crudely chipped stones into the form of axheads and knives;
the neolithic, wherein are found polished stone implements. And
then the Bronze and Iron Ages.

No stones of paleolithic or eolithic character have yet come to
light in China; all of the earliest stone implements so far found
have been polished, many of them elaborately and elegantly. Thus
it is not justifiable to speak of a true stone age in China or a true
stone age of the Chinese people.

So we cannot view the beginning of the craft of jade carving, we can only surmise about it. Nor can we determine when the first man lived who used jade, or where, or who his ancestors were. We can only look back over the course of Chinese civilization and note that there was never a time in recorded history when the Chinese did not carve jade or hold it in special esteem.

Some scholars hold that immediately prior to the Bronze Age in China there occurred a Jade Age, when the principal material used in weapons and implements was nephrite. The evidence, after decades of discussion, remains inconclusive. It seems more important for us to realize that the history of China, as we know it, has been a long, uninterrupted Jade Age. While the Maoris of New Zealand and the Indians of Alaska prized nephrite only until the introduction of metal tools, the Bronze Age in China served to make jade's place firm and permanent. There is no more concrete evidence of the regard in which jade was held by the Chinese than the fact that they reproduced the bronze ceremonial vessels in jade. They knew which substance would survive longest!

The history of China, as we know it, has been a long uninterrupted Jade Age, from the Shang Dynasty . . . Tiger pendant. Pale greenish nephrite. L: 4⅜". H: 1⅜". T: ⅛". Courtesy Art Institute of Chicago, Chicago, Illinois. Edward and Louise B. Sonnenschein collection.

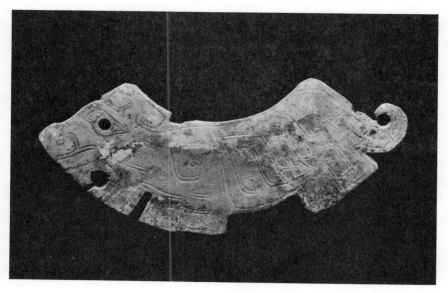

to the twentieth century . . . Excellent modern carving in the thin Tibetan style. Light green nephrite. H: 8″. Courtesy M. H. De Young Memorial Museum, San Francisco, California. Avery Brundage collection.

When China's true history began in the Chou Dynasty (1122 or 1050 B.C.) the art of carving jade was already well established within traditional forms; jade was an indispensable part of court and religious ceremonials, the medium for fine carvings, popular articles of adornment, decorative objects. Going back as far as art remains will take us (before 1050 B.C.), we find jade in all of the Shang tombs, used in a variety of ways. There is every indication that tradition, which recesses another thousand years, is correct in speaking of still more ancient jade.

The Archaeology of Jade

Between its discovery and use by primitive man and our appreciation of it today, the earth reclaimed its treasure.

As early as the Shang Dynasty (*c.* 1766 or 1550 B.C.–1122 or

1050 B.C.) the Chinese buried jade in the tombs with their dead. Ritual objects of worship, utensils, knives, and ornaments of jade were interred with the deceased to accompany them on their trip to the life beyond. For many centuries these objects, preserved by the earth, survived, while those above the ground, retained for use by the living, did not.

We have already mentioned that many of these objects, including token weapons, were so small or so thin as to render them fit only for ceremonial use. Strategically placed holes, grooves, and notches indicate that some might have been worn as emblems of rank or as amulets during the lifetime of the deceased. Others may have served as inlay for wooden objects, which disintegrated in the tombs. The majority were probably carved only as funerary gifts.

All of the archaic jade that exists today came to us by way of the tombs, with thanks due, in part, to the steam-powered locomotive.

Railroads and Grave Robbers

One of the most important, but least considered, dates in the history of Chinese art is A.D. 1876, since it was in this year that the first railroad was built in China.

Until this time the burial sites were held inviolate. To open them, or even knowingly step upon them, would incur the wrath of the ancestors. The sites of the graves of the nobility were often both sacred and secret. Those of the commoners were known but respected; in many parts of China, in a special ceremony each spring, the villagers would go to their family plots and add a prescribed amount of dirt to the grave mounds, so that the oldest grave was indistinguishable from a small hill.

It all happened with a simple geometric certainty. Whenever possible, railroads had to travel in straight lines. There were few places in the populated parts of China where you could draw a straight line for many miles without crossing a grave or a tomb.

For some years the Chinese fought the new means of locomotion. Progress met tradition—by 1905 progress had won. But only in a way, for the subsequent archaeological discoveries enriched the world's knowledge of China's past, revealed the tremendous heritage of its art, and brought to light the story of ancient jade, adding substance to legend and tradition.

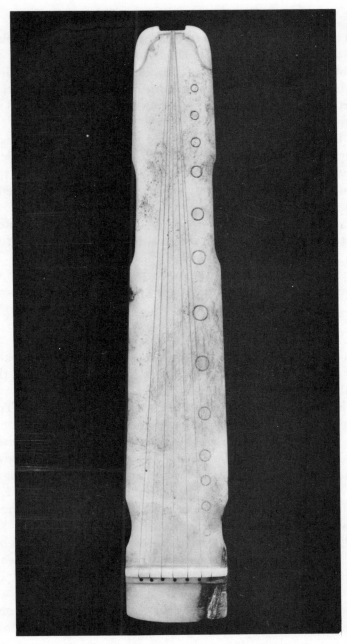

Music for the life beyond . . . Miniature lute, one of the many varieties of tomb jade. Gray nephrite. L: 9″. w: 2″. Ming Dynasty. Courtesy Chicago Natural History Museum, Chicago, Illinois.

Western archaeologists paid well for the newly revealed art remains. Before long, when the news of these finds reached the art world, collectors paid even better. Then, working in conflict with all tradition, the grave robber came onto the scene. Fields were pock-marked with holes as by day the scavengers sought the tombs, probing with long metal rods. By night they would work in teams, excavating the most promising locations, half of them digging, the other half standing guard with weapons. The penalty was death. But the rewards might mean a lifetime of leisure, for such was the worth of jade. Only when a tomb was found and opened would the torches appear, as the men rushed into the moldy gloom, casting greedy, frightened shadows while they grabbed large bronzes, jade censers, powerful but fragile pottery, at the same time trying to avoid looking at the dead, who, contrary to prevailing belief, had not been saved from decomposition by the jade. Grabbing as much as they could carry, they would flee quickly, leaving behind them pieces of broken pottery, a few threads of badly decomposed brocade, overturned vases.

This is a part of the story of the awakening of the world to the long history of Chinese art. For every scientifically excavated tomb—and they were relatively few—dozens were broken into and looted by night. Much of China's artistic heritage was scattered and dispersed under frightened feet. Yet the paramount quality which rendered jade valuable to primitive man was to save most of it in the haphazard foraging: it was the world's toughest stone.

It was also the most valuable to the Chinese. Most of the looted jade quickly made its way onto the market or into private collections. Nearly all of the ancient jade we possess today came to us through the hands of grave robbers or farmers, who sometimes unearthed it while plowing their fields.

The Problem of Dating

The pieces were sold with no questions asked, no information volunteered, for no one was eager to admit to grave robbing. Once separated from the tombs, most jade was nearly impossible to date. Only by examining similar pieces from known tombs and establishing stylistic parallels to other dated art forms, notably bronze, has it been possible to determine the approximate period in which most jade was carved.

Significant Sites

Though ancient jade is said to have been found in a number of places in China, few of these sites were scientifically excavated. Those which were include three in Honan Province: *An-yang,* the capital during the Shang Dynasty, where numerous Shang jades were unearthed; *Shing-Hsiang,* which yielded many flat pieces, delicately carved and polished; and *Chin-Ts'un,* where was found a large number of pendants and small carvings, many of a translucent pale yellow nephrite.

For the nearly two thousand years of the Christian Era there has been a lack of such tombs, essential to proving the age of a piece of jade, with two important exceptions.

One is the tomb of the Emperor Wang Chün, who ruled from

*Only by establishing stylistic parallels with other dated art forms has it been possible to determine the approximate period in which most jade was carved . . . A three-*color dated Ming pottery Lohan. In addition to the over-all form, note the details, especially the folds of the robe and the hair design.

A.D. 907 to 918, during the Five Dynasties period. Opened in 1942, the tomb included a disk, an Imperial seal, and seven large plaques fashioned into a belt.

The Tomb of Wan-li

The tomb of the Emperor Wan-li, excavated in 1956, was more productive, although the Chinese Communist government has not, to date, revealed complete details of the treasures. Wan-li reigned from A.D. 1573 to 1619, and his is the first Ming tomb to be opened scientifically. It seems likely that once the objects are carefully studied the present dating of many art objects will be changed.

In one large square chamber leading to Wan-li's tomb the eave tiles were whole pieces of "sweat white" jade, held together by a stone tablet. The huge door to the tomb and the doors separating the various rooms were made of whole pieces of white jade. Two carved animal heads of jade held the door rings.

Compare this jade carving with the porcelain opposite. While this Lohan could have been carved at a later date, the many similarities indicate it was probably also a product of the Ming Dynasty. Pale green nephrite. H: 10″. Both figures courtesy M. H. De Young Memorial Museum, San Francisco, California. Avery Brundage collection.

The huge door to the Emperor Wan-li's tomb was made of whole pieces of white jade . . .

Surrounding the painted coffins of Wan-li and two of his wives were many treasures; some, such as a porcelain censer, had never before been known to exist. While no catalogue has been published listing the many jades, we do know that among them were two ceremonial tablets (one, engraved with four mountains, was wrapped in a case and placed next to the Emperor's neck), censers, wine jugs (one with the jug, chain, and stopper carved from a single piece of white "mutton fat"), beakers, a white rabbit earring, and the nine ritual body jades.

We hope that the Chinese Communist government will in time reveal details of the tomb and its treasures. This will probably be another important chapter in the story of jade. It may be that some of the objects we attribute to later periods actually date from Ming times.

For example, that both the huge doors and the eave tiles were made of pure-white jade would indicate that an unusually large deposit of fine nephrite was unearthed during this period or earlier.

It would seem logical that many other objects were also carved from the same material. Many of the beautifully carved white jade bowls which we have dated eighteenth or nineteenth century (or Ching)—yet which are carved in shapes also used during the Ming Dynasty—may be Ming or earlier, after all. This is just a sample of the deduction that becomes possible with each new dated discovery.

Further findings can and probably will occur in China, throwing additional light on man's many uses of the stone. Yet archaeology is only one part of jade's story. Archaeological and aesthetic interests are not always synonymous, nor is age the most important criterion of art value.

Some of the finest jade carvings extant were carved during the past one hundred years. Some of the most beautiful jade ever mined first saw light in this century. Perhaps it is fitting that jade is so difficult to classify and date, for it is not a dead but a living stone, "highly charged with creative force," whose story has no discernible beginning or ending in time but will exist as long as the earth houses creatures capable of awakening to its inherent beauty.

With the discovery of the Wan-li tomb, many objects previously dated Ching may very well prove to be Ming or earlier . . . Pure-white nephrite bowl, of a pattern used during and after the Ming Dynasty. H: 3½". D: 8½". Courtesy M. H. De Young Memorial Museum, San Francisco, California. Avery Brundage collection.

CHAPTER THREE

THE WORLD OF JADE

Pi: Symbol of Heaven. Light green nephrite. w: 8⅝″. D: 6½″. Late Chou Dynasty. Courtesy William Rockhill Nelson Gallery of Art, Kansas City, Missouri.

Benevolence lies in its gleaming surface
Knowledge in its luminous quality
Uprightness in its unyieldingness
Power in its harmlessness
Purity of soul in its rarity and spotlessness
Eternity in its durability
Moral leading in the fact that it goes from
hand to hand without being sullied.

"The Book of Rites" (*Li Chi*) on Jade
(Chou Dynasty, 1122 or 1050–256 B.C.)

Now we come to some of the "mysteries" of jade. Among the strangest and most fascinating are those concerning its place in religion.

No other stone has ever played such an important part in religious ritual.

No other stone has had as long an unbroken connection with religion.

No other stone has ever been accorded such devout religious fervor.

Yet, although almost every object in nature was at one time or another worshiped by the Chinese, jade was not. From the beginning of China's recorded history the Chinese attitude toward the stone has remained constant: *Never worshiped, but always revered.*

Perplexing?

With the equation Toughness=Survival=Life=Worship, we have given a probable reason for jade's original connection with religion and its continued use in traditional religious rites. But this does not explain why jade *held* this unique esteem for more than three thousand years, in such divergent philosophies and religions as nature worship, ancestor worship, Shamanism, Confucianism, Taoism, Buddhism, Mohammedanism, and Christianity. Nor does it explain why jade was never worshiped. Nor why the Chinese went to great lengths to prevent this from happening.

Part of the answer lies in the unusual role given jade by the Chinese.

Jade's Special Place

Jade held a special place in Chinese religion, a place accorded no other substance. It was the link between earth and Heaven, the bridge from life to immortality. It was a conduit, a conductor, the embodiment of man's highest thought, just touching upon the divine. In religious ceremonials the Emperor often used jade as we might a telephone, except that when he held up the jade *Pi* form and spoke through it he spoke to Heaven. And through jade, Heaven was said to send its blessings in return.

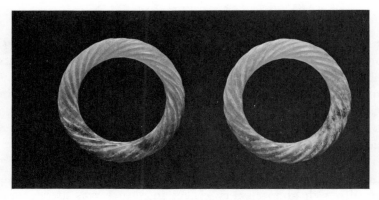

Confucians carried jade to purify the mind, awaken inspiration . . . Small flat rings of translucent yellow-gray and purple nephrite, corrugated spirally. D: 1⅜". Late Chou Dynasty. Courtesy Freer Gallery of Art, Washington, D.C.

"Jade is Heaven," states the "Book of Changes" (*I Ching*), China's oldest and most important work of divination; meaning that with this body and these senses man could conceive no more perfect substance. Confucians carried it to purify the mind, to awaken inspiration. Taoists called it Yang, the male creative principle, since in its purest form it resembled the seed of man and was

Buddhist mystics used it to attain Samadhi . . . White nephrite Buddha.
H: 10″. 18th or 19th century. Courtesy M. H. De Young Memorial Museum,
San Francisco, California. Avery Brundage collection.

said to contain the potentialities of all life, both human and
divine. Buddhist mystics used it to reach the state of Samadhi.

This was jade's special place. But knowing this only brings us
to another, more basic question. *Why jade?*

To begin to answer this, we must first understand the Chinese
relationship to nature, which is, in many ways, basically different
from our own.

NATURE WORSHIP

Viewing the early art of man, we note that the world was divided into two great camps: the Pacific center, which included Alaska, the Americas, Mexico, Formosa, China, Japan, and the various Pacific island groups; and the Western center, embracing the Mesopotamian Plain, the northern Nile Valley, and the Greek Mediterranean.

The difference of attitude in these two camps was significant and was reflected in their art.

In the art of the Western center the focal point was man. Man was the center of the universe. Even his gods resembled him, being part human, part animal, and heroically divine, as exemplified in the sculpture of Egypt and Greece.

Man's fate was to be at eternal odds with nature; his victories, to conquer its forces through sheer will and brute strength, if only for a time. Majestic Prometheus bound on a mountain peak.

In the Pacific center the attitude was different, almost leisurely. No one fought nature. It was easier to move in accord with it. No man cursed nature for his misfortunes. Instead, through additional sacrifice and devotion, he sought to right the imbalance that he had (perhaps unknowingly) caused. In their art the natives of the Pacific center were concerned primarily with honoring or symbolizing the forces of nature. They were devotees of nature rather than of man.

And what was man's place in their scheme of things?

You can discover it if you look closely at a Chinese painting. Where is man? There, that tiny figure sitting on that small bridge, in the midst of that vast landscape which represents the universe.

The Chinese were the first to paint landscapes as landscapes rather than as background for mortals, for they knew nature, respected and worshiped it. In even fewer words, they accepted nature, and in so doing they lived closely attuned to its changing moods.

Psychiatrists today have noted these differences in perspective. They refer to the man who believes that the universe revolves around him, limiting him, frustrating his every endeavor, as "the immature mind." The man who realizes his place in the scheme of things is tabbed "the mature mind."

The Chinese attitude went past mere acceptance of the status quo, however, as is evident in various Chinese religions, whose goals were often the same: to transcend the limited mortal personality and to find in Nirvana, or Tao, or the Spirit, at-one-ment with all nature. In short, to be like jade.

Sacrifice

Close to nature, aware that they were dependent upon it for their very existence, the early Chinese saw in its changes the will of supernatural forces. Each aspect of nature had two faces, its Yang and its Yin. The sun could cause seed to grow or it could parch the land. The rain could give energy to plants or create floods. The new season might bring prosperity or famine. The earth might produce abundance or refuse to yield.

As did primitive peoples in all parts of the world, the Chinese believed that one way to assure the benevolence of the elements was through sacrifice. Long before recorded history began, they chose jade for this special function.

Perhaps, as we have said, it was the toughness of the stone that marked it for this use. Or, again, it may have been its beauty. Possibly, as we shall soon consider, there were other qualities, inherent in the nature of the stone, that made it seem an ideal vehicle for communication with forces greater than man.

Whatever the basic reason, in the earliest known form of Chinese worship we find that Shan and Shui, the deities of hill and stream, were worshiped through the sacrificial use of jade.

Basic Nature Symbols

Today we can look at jade carved thousands of years ago or yesterday and see the place held by nature in Chinese thought. For believing it to be "the quintessence of creation," the very "essence of nature," the Chinese mirrored on its surface, in basic symbols, a microcosm of the universe as they knew it.

Meander   Leaf pattern   Rice-grain pattern   Silkworm pattern

The meander was derived from the clouds overheard. The leaf pattern was symbolic of leaves (and later drawn swords). A field of raised or incised knobs represented the all-important rice grains.

Those with tails, silkworms. The Yang-Yin could be any pair of opposites, but generally was Male-Female or Day-Night.

Yang-Yin

Almost every object or force in nature is to be found in jade symbolism. Trees, flowers, vegetables; mountains, rivers, ocean waves; marine life, insects; thunder, lightning, rain; the sun, the moon, the stars and constellations; the seasons; the four directions.

Color, too, was symbolic of nature, as were many of the fantastic creatures in the animal kingdom (as wonderful a collection of beasties as the mind of man has ever encountered or created), but before venturing into these realms, let's see how even the *forms* of jade carvings were closely related to the world about man.

The Six Ritual Jades

For well over three thousand years, the traditional religious rites of the Imperial court of China were devoted primarily to obeisance to Heaven, through the ritual use of certain objects of jade. The most important of these, the Six Ritual Jades, were also widely used in burial rites.

> *With a sky-blue Pi worship is paid to Heaven.*
> *With a yellow Ts'ung to Earth.*
> *With a green Kuei to the East.*
> *With a red Ch'ang to the South.*
> *With a white Hu to the West.*
> *With a black Huang to the North.*
>   "The Book of Rites" (*Li Chi*)

The Pi and the Ts'ung

The *Pi* (pronounced *bee*) is a flat, round disk with a hole in the center. It represents Heaven.

Pi

The *Ts'ung* is a round cylinder enclosed within a square. It represents earth.

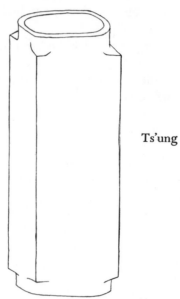

Ts'ung

In tombs the *Ts'ung* form was often placed on the chest or abdomen of the dead, the *Pi* form under the back. Thus the dead rested between Heaven and earth.

The earliest known forms of the *Pi* are plain and roughly cut, probably with crude abrasives. As the art of jade carving progressed, relief carvings first appeared on one side, then on both, until many of the later *Pi* forms were highly ornamented with complex designs and symbols. The *Pi* varies in size from 1 inch to 1 foot across. The width of the center opening is generally one fifth of the total diameter.

To understate the case, there has been a tremendous amount of educated guesswork regarding the origin of this form.

Guesses include: a stone suspended and struck to make ritual music; an astronomical instrument; a wheel; the flywheel of a drill; a bracelet; a circular stone ax; the sun disk; the sun shining through the vault of Heaven; and Heaven itself.

We have only to put ourselves momentarily in the place of these early Chinese and look up to the sky, to see that the last three are the most likely.

As support for what our eyes tell us, John La Plant of Stanford

University notes that "there was no separate word for 'Heaven' in ancient China. The *Pi* was referred to as a symbol for ✷ which is equally *Heaven* and *sky*." As conclusive, visually, is the Chinese character for sun ☉

Whatever its progenitor, by the time of the Han Dynasty (206 B.C. –A.D. 220) the carving on the *Pi* and reference to it in ancient texts coincide sufficiently for us to be sure it was then generally used as a symbol of Heaven.

The origin of the *Ts'ung* form, symbol of earth, has also received its share of conjecture (with the inevitable addition of sexual symbolism).

The proportions of the *Ts'ung* vary greatly, but its form is basically that of a cylinder flanked by four prisms. The four corners of the *Ts'ung* typify the four elements—water, fire, wood, and metal —as well as the earth's four directions. The fifth element, earth, is represented by the *Ts'ung* itself.

One theory has it that the *Ts'ung* was at one time, if not originally, used as a container for the royal ancestral tablets. Another, S. Howard Hansford's, is that it derives from the plan of the ancient tombs. Hansford adds that "certainly a better symbol of Mother Earth could hardly be found than the portal by which her children returned to her bosom." The sexual symbolists remind us that in China, as in most other parts of the world, the earth was considered to be female.

We do know that by Han times the *Ts'ung* was used as a symbol for the earth in conjunction with the Heaven symbol *Pi*.

While the *Pi* is of simple form and could easily have been cut from flat slabs of jade, the *Ts'ung* is evidently the product of a far more highly evolved art. It is quite possible that centuries passed between the fashioning of the first *Pi* and the first *Ts'ung*, and that in the interim the introduction of metal tools, along with newer abrasives, may have taken place. Marks on several early *Ts'ung* would seem to bear this out.

What is definite is that both of these forms were undoubtedly inspired by nature and that both were used to represent it, and to pay respect to it, in ceremonial worship.

The Kuei, Hu, Huang, and Chang

The four other ritual jades represent the four directions and the four seasons. Judging only by the simplicity of their form—all four are flat, tablet-like—they may, like the *Pi*, be older than the *Ts'ung*. In the tombs, these four ritual jades were placed in corresponding positions around the body: the *Kuei* to the left, the *Hu* to the right, the *Huang* above the head, and the *Chang* below the feet.

Kuei

The *Kuei*, traditionally of green jade, was used as a symbol of the East, Imperial Power, and Spring. Its knife-like shape is the best clue to the *Kuei's* original model. A large number of these have been discovered, varying from plain tablets with only a few crossed lines to others with ornate carvings of mountains, the animals in the Chinese zodiac, and the constellations. The Big Dipper is frequently portrayed, in either its natural form, or its artistically stylized form.

The *Hu* is an image of a tiger, usually in white jade, which represents the West and Autumn. In style it has undergone the same basic changes as the other animal representations in Chinese art, from a crude naturalistic form to a more unrecognizable beast of fantasy.

The *Huang* is half a *Pi*, semicircular, usually of black jade, and a symbol of the North and Winter. Later artisans occasionally shaped it to look like a fish or hydra, the dragon of the waters.

The *Chang* tablet is half a *Kuei*. It was made of red jade and was used as a symbol of the South and Summer.

Hu

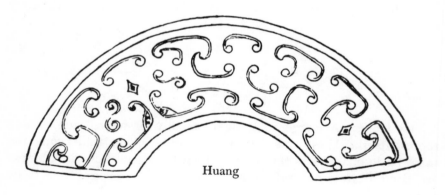

Huang

The Ritual Worship of Heaven

How were these six ritual forms used?

For a change, we don't have to surmise. This ceremony, which was formalized before 1000 B.C., was enacted in all its detail as late as March 1, 1934, when the Japanese-recognized "boy Emperor" Kang Teh ascended the throne of Manchukuo. Despite the passage of three thousand years of Chinese history, its two most prominent features—the worship of Heaven and the use of jade —had never changed.

To visualize this ceremony, once so important to the Chinese state, let's imagine that we are witnesses to this worship as it took place somewhere in China, centuries ago:

All is now in order. Less than a mile from the Imperial camp, a hastily constructed altar of rough stone is set up in the center of the plain. Had he been at home in the capital at the time of the equinox, the Emperor would have made this ritual worship on the grounds of the Imperial Palace. However, on all long journeys, such as this one, he has with him all of the necessities for worship.

The blue canopy over the altar sways gently in the early-morning breeze. A long red crane flies high overhead toward the northern marshes, his trailing call growing fainter, until it blends into the first musical note struck on the jade chimes.

All the members of the court are assembled in their ritual positions around the altar as the Imperial procession comes into view. The long column moves forward in slow rhythm, following the precedent of ancient ancestors, who are now invoked, by the chimes, to pay heed to the ceremonies.

Several yards from the altar, the horses stop and the Emperor alights from the Jade Chariot, the twelve pendants of jade which adorn his royal robes tinkling merrily. These pendants represent the twelve hours in the Chinese day and the twelve yearly cycles of the moon. Only the sovereign can wear them all.

A few feet away, the Chief of the Jade Storehouse lifts from the sedan chair a large red ceremonial box, which as yet is still sealed. This man is guardian of the Imperial treasures, which include gold, ivory, and multitudinous gems, but whose habitation is named after the most precious substance within its walls. When the Emperor makes a long journey the Chief is responsible for the ritual objects of worship.

As the Emperor approaches, the seal is broken, the lid of the box lifted, and the highly polished ritual objects gleam in the bright sunlight. The long flat *Kuei*, the symbol of Imperial Power, without which the Emperor cannot approach the altar, he now takes in his right hand. The circular *Pi* form, of blue-green jade, symbol of Supreme Power and Heaven, he carries in his left.

Again the musicians strike the jade chimes as the Emperor turns and walks solemnly toward the altar, signifying that the worship is to begin. The Chief of the Jade Storehouse follows, two of his assistants bearing the box of ritual jades. The Emperor mounts the altar stairs.

Waiting at the sides of the altar are the nobility; the number and color of the jades they wear, the scepters they carry indicate their respective royal positions. While the Emperor, the Son of Heaven, wears white jades suspended from azure cords, the dukes wear mountain-green jades with red cords, the governor water-green jades with black cords, and the heir presumptive pale green jade with green cords. Here too are the animals to be sacrificed, the knife of jade, and the jade vessels which will hold the offerings and be burned with them. The sacrificial fire is now lit.

The ceremony is long. By the time the Emperor has made offerings of jade to the East, North, West, and South, the animals slaughtered and the wine poured, then offered to Heaven in jade dishes, the sun is high. A bank of clouds floats leisurely overhead, followed by the lone red crane, who again observes the smoke, the geometric lines of men, the colorful banners far below. Perhaps he flies a little more surely now, for the Emperor has once again established peace for all creatures below the heavens.

The Colors of Nephrite

These hues of jade were more than colors to the ancient Chinese.

Five, in their purity, represented nature's basic elements: yellow, earth; black, water; white, air or metal; red, fire; and green, wood. This was on one plane.

On another they were, respectively, earth, the four directions—north, west, south, east—and, adding blue, Heaven.

On still another they represented the influences of Saturn, Mercury, Venus, Mars, and Jupiter.

In their subtlest form, as elemental forces, they combined to make up man and his world. They were the substance of everything terrestrial.

And, certainly not least important, they gave us the many-splendored nature of jade.

This was a living symbolism, the symbolism of color, and though much of it has been forgotten now, we can still re-create moments:

Imagine a small tiger carving of black jade being tossed into the swollen stream to appease the God of Water. Or imagine a farmer carefully placing a broken piece of yellow jade in his field as an offering to the God of Earth because he knows that "if grain grows near jade, it never can be affected by excessive rains or dryness."

We can visualize a Chinese elder on the first day of the new year, caressing his fingering piece of blue and yellow jade, remembering that "the propitious air of heaven and earth is always condensing into jade." And we can experience the joy of the carver, as well as the eventual possessor, on finding that much-coveted combination: the five basic colors in one piece. Or understand how a man, carrying jade of a certain hue, might believe he was attracting the influence of a favored planet.

Though we have lost the keys to the combination of the elemental forces which were said to explain everything in the universe (or perhaps, more accurately, we no longer possess insight into the poetic magic of the ancient "Book of Changes" where these rites are defined), we have not lost their beauty, since it exists yet in the colors of jade.

If you have ever seen a color or imagined one, no matter how distinctive or subtle, know that somewhere it appears in jade. Spend an hour or two in any of the museums housing major jade collections and you will soon discover not only how the colors often determined the shape and nature of a carving but also why the Chinese, in endeavoring to name all the major colors, had to call upon almost every known animal, vegetable, or mineral (sometimes several times) to find fitting designations.

Listing only a few of the most common names: from the animal kingdom came antelope, chicken bone, egg, kingfisher, mutton fat, nightingale, and shrimp; from the vegetable kingdom, apple, bamboo, betel nut, chestnut, chrysanthemum, date, melon, moss, olive, young onion, peach, pine flower, rice, rose, sunflower, and spinach; from the minerals, all the other precious stones, emerald, ivory, pearl, and sapphire.

There are said to be over one hundred distinct shades of green; hundreds more combining green with other colors, such as "moss-entangled-in-snow." The sky and waters provide many more designations for both blues and greens, such as "sky-after-the-rain," "sky-reflected-in-clear-water," "spring-water-green," and "cloud sky."

Some of the names chosen are perhaps *too* descriptive—such as "purple-of-the-veins" and "mucus-of-the-nose-gray." Others especially favored by the Chinese are somewhat less appreciated in the West, such as the lardy yellow "mutton fat." The unusual shades of the calcined, often partially decomposed burial pieces—the rich browns and reds, the old ivory known as "chicken-bone"—are more appealing when we don't know that the Chinese believed that their distinctive hues were caused by contact with the blood and flesh of the deceased.

Pure jade (both nephrite and jadeite) is white. Color comes from the presence of other minerals in the stone, mostly compounds of iron, manganese, or chromium. Iron, in various oxides and silicates, gives the largest variety of hues—pale green, browns and yellows, grays, near black, and, on very rare occasions, blue. Manganese, too, is sometimes responsible for shades of gray and black and, again rarely, pink. The presence of chromium makes possible the vivid emerald-green of Imperial jadeite or jewel jade.

Ancient Chinese scholars might have agreed to but certainly would not have been stopped by this explanation. They claimed there could be no definitive list of jade's colors, that many were so subtle they could not be perceived by the senses of man.

Thus even the colors of the stone played a multi-dimensional role —reflecting nature, participating in its worship, and serving as a bridge to that which lay just beyond the knowledge, though not the imagination, of man.

Animals—Mythological and Actual

In portraying the nature of the world around them, the Chinese did not forget the members of the animal kingdom, who provided inspiration for some of the finest jade carvings known to us. It should not be surprising that, transferred to jade, many were less animalistic than godlike in their attributes, for they too were often symbols or masks for the forces of cosmic change.

Dating from even before the axes and daggers of Shang times (1766 or 1550 B.C.) are a number of full animal carvings in nephrite. For safety's sake we label these crude, naturalistic carvings "neolithic style"; in them we can clearly recognize fish, birds, rams, buffaloes.

Yet we might question whether the ancient craftsmen carved

Mythological or actual? Chimera. White nephrite. H: 2⅜″. L: 3½″. Ch'ing Dynasty. Courtesy Art Institute of Chicago, Chicago, Illinois. Edward and Louise B. Sonnenschein collection.

what they saw for the mere sake of carving, or whether the forms also had symbolical meaning.

Several have advanced theories to explain the importance accorded animals in early Chinese art. One theory has it that these animals were distinguishing symbols of particular clans or family groups, that they probably trace back to a parallel between the qualities of the family's legendary ancestor and the special qualities of a certain beast, such as strength, daring, fleetness, courage. We know that in Chinese myth the line between man and beast is often even less clearly defined. One of the oldest Chinese legends is of the invasion of China by wild beasts, sometime around 2700 B.C., and of how the Yellow Emperor skillfully organized them into an army with which he routed his enemy, Yen Ti. The worship of animals, the currying of their favor, these are all possible explanations for the dominating presence of animals in early Chinese art.

By Shang times, however, when the animals appeared as decorative design on other objects such as the *Pi* and *Kuei*, we may be sure that if they had ever been *merely* animals they were no longer; they now clearly represented forces of nature.

Stag. Green nephrite, discolored to the color and texture of ivory. H: 2⅞″.
L: 1⅞″. Chou Dynasty. Courtesy Metropolitan Museum of Art, New York.
Heber R. Bishop collection.

We know that many animals frequently carved in jade—the horse, fox, tiger, rabbit, bird, bat, fish, toad, and tortoise, to name only the most prominent—were real animals, for they are with us today. But what of the others? Did the *dragon* ever exist? Or the gentle *unicorn?* Or the *phoenix*, the *hydra*, the *lin?*

Were these fabulous beasts of mythology, or actual animals, presented with artistic imagination?

The Dragon

Let us start with the greatest and most notable of Chinese beasts, the dragon. Was he a dim race-memory of an actual animal who lived in the now mythical past, or merely the alligator, which appeared in the river at floodtime to the amazement of the Chinese and hence became known as the bearer of rain?

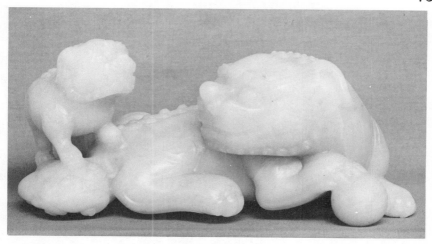

Lions. White nephrite, with light greenish tint. H: 3½″. L: 8¼″. W: 5½″. Ming Dynasty. Courtesy Metropolitan Museum of Art, New York. Heber R. Bishop collection.

Dragon: Guardian of the East, symbol of Spring, courage and imperial sovereignty . . . Grayish-green nephrite. H: 3⅜″. L: 6½″. T: ¼″. Chou Dynasty. Courtesy Art Institute of Chicago, Chicago, Illinois. Edward and Louise B. Sonnenschein collection.

Whatever his origin, it was not long before he represented a cosmic force and was worshiped accordingly. By Han times (206 B.C.–A.D. 220) the dragon was the Guardian of the East, a symbol

Transformations of the dragon:

of Spring, courage, Imperial sovereignty. From his mouth at various times came royal edicts, prophecies, proclamations of Heaven, fire, and the clouds which contained rain. Studying the dragon form alone, we can trace in detail the major changes in the art of design over the centuries, as the fabulous beast weaves its way in and out of simple forms, geometric abstractions, complicated scrollwork, coats of arms. The art of carving dragons was so basic to China that around A.D. 500, when Liu Hsieh wrote his great work of literary criticism, he could call it "The Literary Mind and the Carving of Dragons" without overlaboring the analogy.

Because of the special qualities attributed to it, the dragon became in Taoist times the embodiment of Yang, the male force, even as jade. Unlike the Western dragon, who was nearly always evil, with a propensity for kidnaping fair maidens, the Eastern dragon was capable of great good if one would treat him reverently. Perhaps all he really wanted was respect.

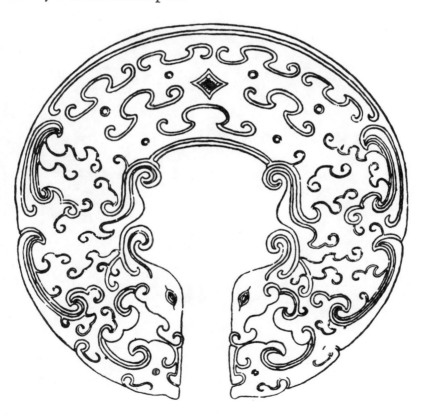

The Hydra

The hydra is assumed by many to have been derived from the dragon. In early carvings their chief difference was that the hydra had a double tail. The hydra's dominions were oceans and rivers; he was the dragon of the waters. Sacrifices of flat pieces of jade, with a dragon carved upon them, were made to the rivers by travelers eager to placate the River God. Failure to comply with this practice provides the basis for numerous tales in ancient histories. A similar piece of jade was sacrificed on altars to bring rain.

Dragon Bones

The dragon, at some point in prehistoric days, gained the power of flight, befitting its role as Yang, or Spirit. Not all dragons were able to make this transition, however. Dragon bones, found in the

Hydra: Dragon of the Waters . . . Dish decorated with five hydras. Grayish-white nephrite. D: 8¼". Sung Dynasty. Courtesy Metropolitan Museum of Art, New York. Heber R. Bishop collection.

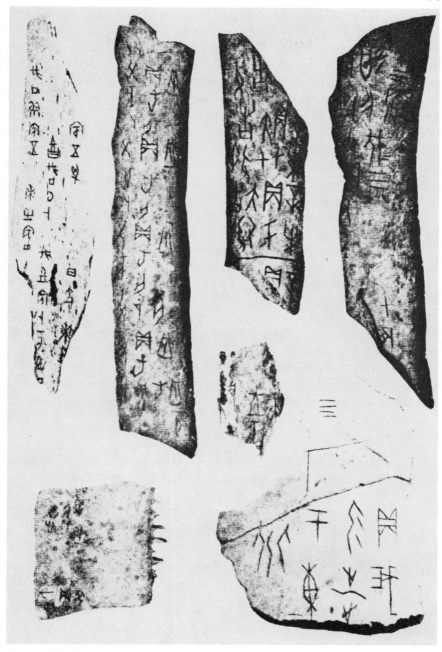

Practical businessmen, the apothecaries knew dragons should have no writing on their bones . . .

soil of China and credited with fantastic medicinal properties, are ascribed by legend to dragons who, lacking the elements of rain and clouds, were unable to ascend majestically. These "dragon bones" were the cause of the greatest single discovery in Chinese archaeology, the finding of the remains of the Shang Dynasty (1766 or 1550 B.C.–1122 or 1050 B.C.), previously considered only legendary which occurred in the late nineteenth century.

Farmers uncovered thousands of these bones while plowing their fields and later sold them to apothecaries. In reality they were Shang oracle bones, used, as was some jade in Shang times, for purposes of divination. A question would be carved upon the bone —"Will the crops be good this year?" or "How many soldiers should I have before I attack the opposing army?" The bones would then be heated and the answer read from the cracks in the substance.

Practical businessmen, the apothecaries knew dragons should have no writing on their bones, so they carefully scraped them clean before selling them. Not until late in the last century did a Chinese antiquarian recognize the ancient script. An exciting treasure hunt followed as archaeologists hastened to purchase all of the bones that had been unearthed. Adding to their problem of deciphering the strange oval notches was the fact that once the value of the bones became known several creative Chinese in the vicinity of the find made their own marks on uncarved bones and put them on the market; the fraud caused many a learned brow to furrow.

The Phoenix

Many animals in China have indiscriminately traded features, giving us winged tigers, pheasants with human faces, and the

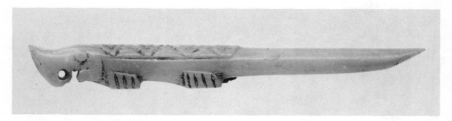

Shang fish knife. Berthold Laufer believed the pointed end of this object was used as a stylus to carve questions on the oracle bones. Others have surmised it was used as a knot opener. White nephrite. L: 3½". Courtesy Chicago Natural History Museum, Chicago, Illinois.

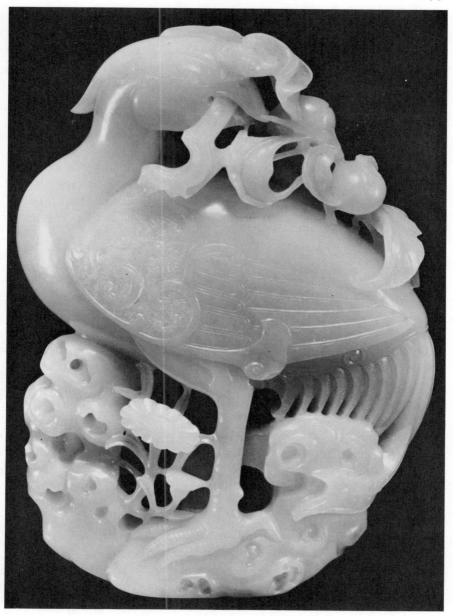

Phoenix: He appears only in times of peace, and will alight only on a
boulder of jade . . . Ornament in the form of a phoenix, conforming to the
shape of the original white nephrite boulder. H: 6⅛″. 18th century. Courtesy
Seattle Art Museum, Seattle, Washington. Eugene Fuller collection.

phoenix, described in one text as resembling "a wild swan fore and a unicorn aft."

Like the dragon, the phoenix was male, Yang, and reputed to be of solar origin. Referred to in ancient texts as early as 2600 B.C., the phoenix is said to live in the fabled Vermilion Hills and to appear among the habitations of man infrequently, only in times of peace. Once here, he will alight only on a boulder of jade. Were the phoenix a little more real and peace a little more prevalent, this might be a good way to find jade.

The presence of the phoenix on princely robes and jade carvings denotes peaceful, auspicious government. Small phoenixes, carved from jade pebbles, are given to young girls upon the attainment of maidenhood.

The Unicorn

While the hydra has domination over the waters and the phoenix over the birds of the air, first among the mammals inhabiting land is the unicorn.

The unicorn is world-renowned. God mentioned it to Job in the Old Testament. We know how it "fought the lion all around the town" on the British royal arms. Not until the nineteenth century did European naturalists realize it was mythological rather than actual.

In China the unicorn is known as the *ki-lin* (*ki* being the male, *lin* the female). It is probably the gentlest of mythological beasts, walking ever carefully lest it damage a blade of grass or another living creature. Its tread is so light that it can walk on water as well as on land. Appearing first as a jade carving in the Han Dynasty, it is considered the incarnate essence of the five elements. Its single horn (the only feature which distinguishes it from actual beasts of the time) is said to possess miraculous powers, not the least among them its properties as an aphrodisiac.

The unicorn has played an important part in Chinese legend. It appears to men only to convey revelations or to announce the birth or death of a great man.

It is said that the Emperor Fu Hsi, who is said to have lived about 2800 B.C., was sad because he had no way of conveying his philosophy of life to his descendants. As he sat musing by the side of a stream, a unicorn appeared; on its back were written the

Unicorn: Gentlest of all mythological beasts . . . Unicorn bearing sacred books. White nephrite. H: 4″. W: 4½″. 18th or 19th century. Courtesy M. H. De Young Memorial Museum, San Francisco, California. Avery Brundage collection.

Eight Mystic Trigrams, which gave Fu Hsi the basis for the Chinese language and later played a prominent part in Taoism.

We have already mentioned how a unicorn appeared to the mother of Confucius, foretelling his entrance into the world. Another heralded his exit. When Confucius was in his seventieth year a unicorn was again seen in the land. When a follower told him of this the great sage looked stricken, cried out, "For whom have you come?" then turned away and sadly sighed, "My teaching is dead." Confucius was neither a superstitious nor an unusually vain man, but he knew an omen when he heard of one. He therewith ceased writing and within two years gave up his body.

Who dares say these animals no longer exist? Vase with dragon handles, ornamented with climbing hydras. Chicken-bone nephrite. H: 4½″. 20th century. Courtesy M. H. De Young Memorial Museum, San Francisco, California. Avery Brundage collection.

Who dares say that these animals no longer exist? Trapped for countless centuries in the remarkable structure of jade, given freedom, a vibrant magic, a majestic motion by the native artists, they live again in man's response to them. The fire-breathing Chimera, the Sing-Sing (whose weakness was wine), the eerie Spirit Fox, the sea monster Kiau are only a few of the wondrous beasts, born of the meeting of imagination and reality, immortalized in the stone of immortality.

Plate 5 Bowl. "Liu's jade," discovered near Sinkiang, Russia, then transported to China for carving. Nephrite. H: 4½″. w at handles: 12¼″. D: 8¼″. Courtesy Lizzadro Museum of Lapidary Arts, Elmhurst, Illinois. Mr. and Mrs. Joseph F. Lizzadro collection.

Almost every beast that walked, swam, crawled, or flew was, during the long course of Chinese art, caught in jade (except the unpopular bird with two pupils in each eye, who fed on jade). They were a part of nature, had a place in the complex scheme of things. Quite often within the simple form of a creature was a wealth of detailed symbolism. The tiger, in addition to its ritual meaning, was a female demon of darkness, guardian of the graves. The bat was a symbol for happiness, since in the Chinese language the words for both had highly similar sounds. Often an animal was not what it pretended to be, but rather a nature spirit, or genii, or sometimes an ancestor assuming animal form. Alfred Salmony, in his *Carved Jade of Ancient China*, states that it is "highly improbable that any figurative representation in early Chinese antiquity was ever without symbolical meaning."

The Forest, the Trees, and the Nature of Jade

What did they symbolize? Nature—the world as the Chinese saw it or believed it to be.

There are texts much thicker than this book which have attempted to catalogue all of the meanings of each symbol; there are art-appreciation-course scholars who can talk glibly of the hidden symbolism of each minute detail of a carving—yet both often lose sight not only of the beauty of the whole carving but of the real purpose of these symbols, which is to reveal the aspects of nature. It is nature which lies behind the symbol; the symbol itself is only the window or special lens through which we look.

Rather than being able to expound eloquently on the thirty-two double-entendres of the dragon symbol, it seems to me much more important for us to become aware that for the first two thousand years Chinese jade carving was essentially a native art, that its symbols and forms were primarily derived from and representative of nature, and that this attitude toward nature in the craftsman's approach to jade is apparent even today.

Jade carving differs from other arts, just as jade differs from other stones. Jade was believed to be the essence of creation; all that existed was believed to be latent, embodied in the stone itself. The craftsman in bronze, the landscape painter, the ceramic potter used their arts to *portray* life as they saw it within traditional forms. But the attitude of the jade carver was different. He did not seek to convey a philosophy, but to *reveal* it. He didn't carve jade to be the master of the world's toughest stone, nor to impose his own order upon the material. He carved to *bring out* the symbols of nature, the patterns of the universe which were *inherent* in jade. Or, as one modern jade artisan has expressed it, "Our job is to subtract; we cannot add."

The stone itself was largely responsible for this approach. Its flaws, veins of various colors, and uneven texture impelled the jade carver to see its latent possibilities for carving. One piece might make either a hideous vase or a number of beautiful small ornaments. Everything hinged upon his awareness of its potentialities. He had to see in the uncarved stone what nature had left there for him.

There is a jade story which serves to illustrate this point.

One of the Ming emperors was offered as tribute an unusually fine piece of nephrite, white with traces of green. He sent the stone to the foremost jade artist in the land, instructing him to carve from it a dragon fighting two Fo dogs.

For several months the artist did not reply. Finally there came a cryptic message requesting his release from the Imperial command. Called before the court to explain his effrontery, the carver simply stated that he was sorry but there was no dragon in the stone, nor any dogs, only four carp swimming lazily through the green weeds in the pool of the Celestial Palace.

Though his advisers suggested punishment, the wise Emperor returned the piece of jade to the craftsman and told him to carve what he perceived. Two years later the man returned with his exquisite carving of the four silver carp. From his pocket he extracted a small pouch in which was contained the excess jade taken from the stone. There was not enough dust to cover the palm of the Emperor's hand.

CHAPTER FOUR

THE STONE OF IMMORTALITY

When I smite my jade musical stone
Be it gently or strong,
Then do the foremost hearts leap for joy
Then do the chiefs agree among themselves.
When ye make to respond the stone melodious,
When ye touch the lyre which is called ch'in,
Then do the ghosts of ancestors, having pleasure
in sweet sounds
Approach to hear . . .

Attributed to the Emperor Yao
of the Legendary Hsia Dynasty
?–1766 B.C.

Musical stone. One of a set of twelve used in Imperial ceremonies. These
were hung by cords from the crossbeam of an upright frame and struck with
a mallet to accompany the recitation of the odes. This piece is also unusual in
that it is a dated jade, carved in the twenty-ninth year of the Emperor Ch'ien
Lung (1765). Gray-green nephrite. Measurements of the six sides: 4 9/16",
13½", 8⅞", 6¾", 5½", 9¼". Courtesy Irwin Eisenberg.

The Other Worlds of Jade

Nature worship was China's first religion. And, in a sense, it has never lost this early prominence. For while China throughout its long history has been "converted" to several major foreign religions and a host of native philosophies, many basic beliefs of early China have never been altered. Reverence for nature is one of these constants. Respect for jade is another.

The Chinese has long accepted his world as one of duality and change. A nature god who is powerful today may be unable to save the harvest next fall, while yet another god, invoked at the last moment, will turn the trick. This does not mean that the Chinese forsakes his earlier deity; he merely relegates it to a somewhat lesser position in the scheme of things. Jade has slipped from eminence in Chinese esteem on only a few occasions, then only officially and never for very long.

We might reason that jade has a subconscious place in Chinese thought. There is evidence that it still retains its hold on the imaginations of many of the Chinese people today—and will probably continue to do so under any regime, as long as the people have access to it.

For jade is no ordinary stone.

Many are its faces. While certain qualities of jade have always been recognized, a number of religions and modes of thought mirrored themselves in jade, seeing within the stone qualities and attributes peculiar to their own vision. Though most had a common awareness of jade's beauty, distinction from other stones, and unusual place in nature, each viewer approached it from a different angle and saw in it a different world.

Who can say which view is correct? Or who can say that this, and nothing more, is the world of jade?

I. ANCESTOR WORSHIP AND JADE

No one knows how ancestor worship began.

Some surmise it started with a dream, the apparition of a person known to be dead; others, that it was a response to the belief of most of us that death cannot be the end.

Contrary to popular opinion, it is a practice not peculiarly Chinese but common to many civilizations. More than 100,000 years ago, Neanderthal man put stone axes and scrapers into the graves of his dead for use in a future life. Nor, evidence duly considered, was it an outgrowth of reverence for the departed. Fear may have been the foundation for what later developed into respect. In some cults the feet of the dead were bound to prevent their roaming and disturbing the living.

Ancestor worship reached China late, perhaps about 10,000 B.C., and stayed long; today it presents innumerable, perhaps unsolvable, problems for the Chinese Communists. While other civilizations in time discarded it, China thoroughly assimilated it, not only in the context of religion, but in the fabric of everyday life and thought.

In conjunction with nature worship, ancestor worship may have been a part of the original religion of China. *Shang-Ti,* the word which during and after the Chou Dynasty (1122 or 1050 B.C.–256 B.C.) meant "Heaven" or "God," may have originally meant the sacrifice made by the Shang Dynasty rulers to their "first progenitor," inasmuch as the pictograph for *Ti* meant both "ruler" and "sacrifice." From the beginning of what we know as Chinese civilization, jade had been inseparably linked with the observance of ancestor worship.

Jade for the Dead

Above ground, as the ritual observance of ancestor worship became formalized, the Chinese built ancestral halls where the spirits of the departed were represented by ancestral tablets of jade. Here the living came when they needed counsel, since through these tablets the communion between earth and Heaven occurred. Marriages, births, deaths, the failure or success of a crop or an army—they spoke of all these things before the tablets. Here, too, periodically and on special occasions, they made sacrifice, often of jade objects.

Below ground, they attempted to provide the dead with every comfort enjoyed in life, plus certain items essential to their peculiar estate. The variety of jade objects extends from arm rests to cooking utensils, elaborate censers to brush handles, ornaments to seals of state, chimes to flutes, ear plugs to phallus preservers.

Tomb jades may be divided into three groups: (1) those jades which might once have been used by the living—for example, vessels and other utilitarian objects; (2) those ritual jades which, to quote John Goette in his *Jade Lore,* "were intended to provide the deceased with a suitable equipment for worship when, through the powers of this sacred stone, he entered into life everlasting in the world beyond," including the *Pi,* the *Ts'ung,* and the Four Cardinal Points; and (3) those specialized objects intended only for use by the dead.

This last group includes shroud weights, armrests, and the jades used to close the nine apertures of the body. As one ancient text put it: "Jade cannot prevent the living from dying, but it can preserve the corpse from decaying." Since the tombs were sacred, never again to be opened, who knew differently?

These nine corpse jades varied considerably in color, shape, and carving.

Often there was placed in the mouth (together with rice) an amulet in the form of a cicada. The cicada was a favorite subject for the jade craftsman, for in three simple stages, from larva to chrysalis to winged insect, it typified resurrection.

The cicada typified resurrection . . . Mottled green and brown nephrite. L: 2¼". W: 1 1/16". T: 3/16". Han Dynasty. Courtesy Art Institute of Chicago, Chicago, Illinois. Edward and Louise B. Sonnenschein collection.

Another tomb jade, used as an eye cover . . . Brown nephrite. L: 2". W: 1¼". Chou Dynasty. Courtesy of Brooklyn Museum, Brooklyn, New York. Mr. and Mrs. Bradley Martin collection.

Plate 6 Demon mask. Shang Dynasty. (1766–1122) B.C. Nephrite. H: 1⅞″.
W: 1½″. T: ¼″. Courtesy Freer Gallery of Art, Washington, D.C.

Plate 7 Ju-I scepter. Ming Dynasty (A.D. 1368–1644) Nephrite. L: 18″.
Courtesy M. H. De Young Memorial Museum, San Francisco, California.
Avery Brundage collection.

When human sacrifice ceased, objects of stone, clay, and jade provided substitutes for the tomb . . . Full-round figure of a kneeling prisoner. Soft blackish stone (not jade). H: 7¾". W: 3½". Chou Dynasty. Courtesy Art Institute of Chicago, Chicago, Illinois. Edward and Louise B. Sonnenschein collection.

A circular jade closed the navel, sometimes with a tiger carved on top to represent the Yin or female force. The ear stoppers bear a close resemblance to those used for the same purpose by the Indians of Central and South America and Mexico. We need not be too explicit about the womb stoppers and phallus preservers, except to note that the latter were often quite realistically carved.

In addition to these nine standard objects, some tombs included various additional body jades, such as chest protectors and knee covers. Also frequent in tombs from the Han Dynasty on were solid little animal charms carved in the round.

These corpse jades are highly prized as amulets by modern Chinese collectors, since there is a belief that they confer long life to their new owners.

A familiar figure in the pre-Christian tombs is Weng Chung, the ancestor. Usually portrayed in the simplest possible style, with slits for eyes and mouth and incised lines to indicate his ornaments, he was later to be claimed by the Taoists as an early incarnation of their founder, Lao-tse.

Human Sacrifice

The first Emperor of Ch'in, who died in 210 B.C., was the last ruler to make the grand exit, his entire harem accompanying him to the grave. It had been the custom earlier to bury the wives and servants of a deceased lord with him when he died. In one tomb near Anyang more than one thousand slaves accompanied their owner to the great beyond. In another tomb eighteen horses and a chariot were found. Human sacrifice ceased during the Han Dynasty, objects of stone, clay, and jade being substituted for both animals and human beings. By the time of the T'ang Dynasty (A.D. 618–907) the tombs were miniature worlds, containing in representation almost everything of consequence the dead had needed while living. We know well the sensitive pottery of this period, the spirited horses, the dignified court figures, the graceful musicians. Many of these objects were also fashioned of jade.

The Radiant Mirror

Ancestor worship was not a one-way proposition. If the heirs showed the proper ritual respect and obeisance, the ancestor in turn was obligated to his descendants. Protection, good weather, health, prosperity, a bountiful harvest—all came from beyond.

Plate 8 Snuff bottle. 18th century. Nephrite. H: 3″. Author's collection.

Plate 9 Vases. 20th century. Jadeite. H: 14¾″ without stands. Author's collection.

The Emperor decided to make his great-grandmother Majestically Beautiful
. . . Set of jade tablets of dark green nephrite, ordered carved by the
Emperor Tao Kuang. Three of the tablets are in Chinese, five in Manchu, with
two additional cover tablets of dragon design. L: 11½″. W: 5″. T: ⅜″. Dated
January 14, 1821. From the author's collection.

Because it was the link between the two worlds, jade often
served as conduit, both to transmit one's worship and to return
the favors of the ancestors.

For example, in 1821, the Emperor Tao Kuang decided to
confer upon his deceased great-grandmother, the consort of
Emperor Yung Chêng, an additional posthumous title, *Majestically
Beautiful*. He did this by having his proclamation carved on a
set of jade tablets in both Manchu and Chinese, inlaid with gold
leaf. His proclamation ends as follows:

This purest gold, resplendent in its beautiful color, will cause our house's felicity to overflow in its perennial freshness, and the flowery jade carved in fragrant designs will elevate our thoughts toward her sacred spirit as we take shelter in its sinuosities.

We earnestly pray that they may continue as her refulgent mirror bringing down manifold prosperity.

So, reverently, have I spoken!

Accept No Substitutes

Often, we know, especially in the cases of emperors and empresses, the jades sacrificed in their honor or accompanying them to the land beyond were the finest obtainable; however, this was not always the case. As evidence that the funerary objects (*Ming-chi*) were sometimes not of the highest quality, we have the following statement in the "Book of Rites" (*Li Chi*): "To treat the deceased as if they were still alive is to lack wisdom." The appended remark of a later commentator is even more blunt and explicit: "All the objects serving as offerings must be imperfect and defective."

The practice of using poor jades for burial purposes was so common by the time of the T'ang Dynasty that an imperial edict was issued. The edict, which might well have been headed *Accept No Substitutes*, or *Quality, Not Quantity, Preferred*, stated that "a virtuous man should not make objects intended to honor the spirits or gifts for the ancestral temple from a substitute material. He should not consider the expense on such an occasion. Jade for votive purposes should be chosen from that of the best quality; one should rather recur to a smaller stone than to a large, inferior one."

Jade has never been a "common" material. We should not be surprised that the Chinese were practical as well as reverent. What is surprising is the artistic merit of even the earliest tomb-jade carvings. The flowing lines, the balance of the mass, the sure, firm designs of the craftsmen, ideally befitting the natural contours of the stone, cause one to wonder whether the gift from Heaven was not as much the art of its carving as the beautiful stone itself.

II. A STONE FOR THE LIVING: CONFUCIUS AND JADE

Had we been in the right place in China at the right time during the sixth century B.C., we would have heard the following conversation:

"How does one best serve his ancestors?" a disciple asked.

"You are not yet able to serve men," the Master answered sharply, but without malice, "how can you serve spirits?"

Again the persistent disciple spoke up, this time asking about death. And Confucius answered, "You do not yet understand life; how can you understand death?"

Contained in this conversation is not only Master Kung's attitude toward life but also his approach to jade.

Confucius was not a religious teacher; he persistently avoided answering questions about life after death, the existence of Heaven, or the efficacy of ancestor worship. He was primarily a thinker, concerned with constructing a system of ethical thought which would be as valid to those who survived him as to his contemporaries. He based his premises not on Heaven but on the nature of the human being. And so he discovered in jade not the mystique of many of his predecessors and descendants but a symbol of the wise man who cultivated his virtues and admitted his faults, thereby making the most of them. To support these comparisons, he quoted "The Book of Verse": "When I think of a wise man, his merits appear to be like jade." And added, "And that is why the wise set so great store by jade . . ."

A Flaw May Be Ground Away

Often he used jade to illustrate examples of ethical conduct:

Be cautious of what you say.
Be reverentially careful of your outward demeanor.
A flaw in a mace of white jade
May be ground away,
But for a flaw in speech
Nothing can be done.

And in the "Book of the Meaning of Sacrifices" (*Li I*):

A filial son will move as if he were carrying a jade symbol, or bearing a full vessel. Still and grave, absorbed in what he is doing, he will seem as if he were unable to sustain the burden, and in danger of letting it fall.

Though his treatises and commentaries on the classics were in time to become law, with most of his interpretations of ritual sacrifice and the use of jade becoming incorporated into court ritual, Confucius never stated his own opinion on the effectiveness

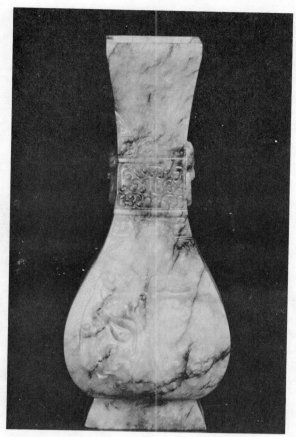

"*A filial son will move as if bearing a full vessel . . .*" Vase. Gray nephrite with streaks of black. H: 8″. W: 3½″. D: 1¼″. Ming Dynasty. Courtesy M. H. De Young Memorial Museum, San Francisco, California. Avery Brundage collection.

of sacrifice. He implied that it was prescribed and therefore should be practiced. He did speak out strongly against sacrifice as barter; all too common was the attitude that costly offerings should bring proportionate favors from on high. And it was largely due to his influence that human sacrifice was eventually abolished in China, which in time, though Confucius had not intended it, added even more jade to the tombs.

Jade, in all of Confucius' references to it, was a stone for the living.

Cool Jade

The Master was himself an accomplished musician on jade chimes. Accredited to his time also was the origin of the practice of using "fondling pieces" of jade. Small jade stones of pleasing color and contour, often uncarved, were carried on the person. The feel of the "cool jade" was said to elevate and purify the thoughts, to quiet the mind and induce a state of contemplation. As years passed, the frequently handled stone would grow even more beautiful in sheen.

As far as Confucius was concerned, jade was a stone for the living . . .
Ornaments. Two belt buckles of green, white, and black nephrite. L: 5¾". W: 1". Archer's thumb ring. Light green nephrite. H: 1". D: 1⅛". Pendant. Green nephrite. D: 2¼". 17th or 18th century. Courtesy William Rockhill Nelson Gallery of Art, Kansas City, Missouri.

Jade is cool to the touch because it is a nonconductor. Confucius would have been pleased with this simple scientific explanation. Most of his contemporaries, however, preferred more magical or poetic explanations; for example, "Jade is cool because it comes from the essence of clear mountain streams."

Scholars and Archers' Rings

In the society into which Confucius was born nobility was hereditary. Warriors (unlike in Japan) were not highly regarded, and few were immortalized in jade. This honor was chiefly accorded the scholars, who in Chinese esteem ranked second only to gods and goddesses.

The unique position of the scholar is part of the fascinating story of jade, for it was the jade archer's ring which marked the scholar's rise to eminence.

Originally the ring was worn on the archer's left thumb to afford protection against the release of the bowstring.

The scorekeeper in archery contests was a specially trained servant who kept score by means of wood or bamboo tallies. Chosen for his intelligence, he was the original *shih*, or writer, and his appointment raised him high above the other servants. H. G. Creel, in *The Birth of China*, tells us: "As writing developed there were other records to be kept, and the *shih* naturally took this duty upon himself. As these records developed into history, the *shih* became a historian. As learning developed, he became a scholar.

"Gradually the scholar rose to a place of power and influence. He was given lands, a fief, in lieu of salary for his services." Eventually, Creel concludes, "there developed the situation whereby, in later Chinese government, virtually all power rested in the hands of the scholars."

To indicate his new position as *shih*, the servant was allowed to wear the jade thumb ring of the archer. Long after the bow, arrow, and archer had become obsolete (until well into the seventeenth or eighteenth century), Chinese scholars continued to wear the jade ring as an emblem of prestige.

III. TAOISM AND JADE: FOOD FOR THE IMMORTALS

Confucianism gained prominence in China because its ethical system of thought was founded on existing human conditions; it appealed to the reason. Taoism gained adherents because it too developed from a strong undercurrent in man, not so much of thought as of feeling, since its basis was nature worship.

Confucius related jade to human virtue. Morally pleasing as this may have been, the Chinese soul demanded a great deal more of the stone of Heaven. The Taoists saw in it what had also long existed there, the elements of beauty, magic, and romance. And they filled this need to overflowing, attributing to jade a complex mysticism surpassing the homage accorded any other stone.

Tao: The Way

Tao was The Way, the path beyond the dualities, the essence of that which was neither and both. Unnamable, undefinable, illimitable, Tao created, permeated, yet was beyond all form. To live in

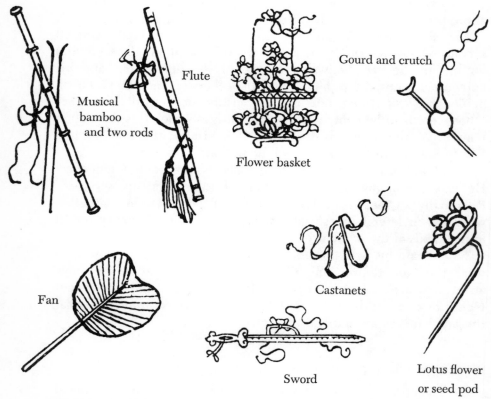

Musical bamboo and two rods

Flute

Flower basket

Gourd and crutch

Fan

Castanets

Sword

Lotus flower or seed pod

Eight Taoist Emblems

accord with Tao was to be in harmony with the essence of nature, yet affectionately detached. In its pure form, as taught by Lao-tse and Chuang-tse, Taoism aimed at regaining the natural simplicity, order, and harmony of the universe within oneself and hence in relation to others. In short, simply *to be*. Tao dealing as it did with elemental powers and the forces of nature, the road to this state of being was beset with some powerfully tempting bypaths. Immortality was one; alchemy and magic were others.

And what was more appropriate to these uses than jade, the essence of Yang, the closest approximation to the Tao that could be contained in material form?

So jade became the alchemist's stone, a source of divination, the pill of immortality. One might note realistically that it is doubtful whether any other stone could have played all these parts so well.

Food for the Immortals

Powdered jade, when taken internally, the ancient texts tell us, would cure everything from insomnia to flatulence. It would prolong life; convey powers of invisibility, levitation, and other more practical feats, such as preventing a person from being thrown from his horse; but, most important, if consumed in quantity it could confer immortality. Worn upon the person (you will recall the origin of our word *jade* a dozen centuries and an ocean away), it not only healed physical ailments but warded off evil, misfortunes, and mischievous supernatural entities. With jade in hand the shamans could conjure up any manner or number of grotesque beings.

Not wishing to decry jade's powers, we must nevertheless note that by reason of its rarity and the loose use of the word *yü* (and the absence of immortal beings), it is probable that, outside royal circles, apothecaries passed off other substances under the misnomer *jade*.

One of the many references to jade's particular properties occurs in the *Botanical Canon of Shen-Nung*, where it is stated that "spiritual and immortal beings, when they were on the point of departing this earth, swallowed five pounds of solution of jade, with this effect, that for three succeeding years their color did not undergo any alteration." To this we can only add that if this solution was really jade it probably hastened their departure as well.

Before we scoff too knowingly, however, we might mention that in addition to the Chinese, the ancient peoples of Central and

South America, Mexico, Alaska, New Zealand, Turkestan, and Persia —strictly coincidentally—attributed to jade the same power to confer immortality.

The Pure August Jade Emperor

Prior to the introduction of Buddhism in the first century A.D., the deity was never represented in human form in China. But the native Taoists were quick to assimilate this new form of worship into their own. A Triad of Gods was created, the most important being the Pure August Jade Emperor, Yü Huang Shang Ti, who became so popular that the Buddhists in time also adopted him.

The Jade Emperor dwelt in the Jade Castle of Abstraction, high above the earth and the thirty-three heavens, according to some

Chung-li Ch'uan, leader
of the Eight Immortals

Chang Kuo-lao,
the magician

accounts; or, according to others, on the Mountain of Jade in the K'un Lun range. Here, on the shore of the Jade Lake, grew a Jade Tree, which measured three hundred arm lengths across and whose red jade fruit conferred the boon of eternal life.

The Eight Immortals

On Clear Jade, a nearby peak, lived the Eight Taoist Immortals. Through the practice of Chinese Yoga and the mastery of nature, these eight gained everlasting life.

They are: their leader, Chung-li Ch'uan, fat, usually with a bare midriff, carrying a peach (a symbol of immortality) in one hand and a whisk fan (to awaken the dead) in the other; Chang Kuo-lao, a magician, who can with equal ease become invisible or compress the white mule he usually rides into wallet size when it isn't needed;

Ts'ao Kuo-chiu, patron of the theater

Lu-Tung-pin, hermit-scholar

Ts'ao Kuo-chiu, patron of the theater, dressed in court robes; Lu-Tung-pin, hermit-scholar, who carries a sword to rid the world of evil; Han Hsuang-tze, patron saint of musicians, whose emblem is the flute and who gained immortality not by eating the magic peach but by falling from the peach tree; and Li T'ieh-kuai, the crippled beggar, usually seen leaning on his staff.

For his tribulations, Li T'ieh-kuai deserves more than passing mention. Once summoned by Lao-tse to the Celestial Regions, he entrusted the care of his body to a disciple, then departed in spirit form. When his absence became prolonged, the disciple, thinking him dead, burned the body. Li T'ieh-kuai eventually returned and, discovering the error, took the closest body at hand, which happened to be that of a lame beggar.

The two remaining Immortals are women: Lan Ts'ai-hao, who

Han Hsuang-tze,
patron of musicians

Li T'ieh-kuai,
the crippled beggar

usually wears a blue gown and wanders about the streets with one foot bare, singing sad melodies; and Ho Hsien-ku, who became a spirit through eating the magic peach, later an immortal through consuming pearl and moonbeams. Sometimes with the Eight Immortals, and often appearing separately, is Lao-tse himself, who usually is pictured as an old man with a long beard sitting astride a water buffalo.

John Goette, in his book *Jade Lore*, calls our attention to the fact that only those Taoist personages who were *not* worshiped appear in early jade carvings. The Pure August Jade Emperor is usually portrayed in wood or lacquer, while the Eight Immortals are a favorite subject of jade artists. This was only one of the safeguards the Chinese took to assure that jade itself was not mistakenly worshiped, that it retain its special role as intermediary.

Lan Ts'ai-hao,
singer of sad songs

Ho Hsien-ku,
who ate her way to immortality

The Magic Elixir of Eternal Life

The Taoists' obsession with longevity and immortality led them to assign symbolical meanings to many objects. Among those which frequently appear on jade carvings are the peach, pine trees, bats, deer, the tortoise, whisks, cranes, rabbits, toads, and the moon.

Two interesting variations of the same legend, often carved in jade, connect the rabbit, the toad, and the moon with immortality. In both the principal figure is a woman known as Heng O.

In one story it is said that Heng O, having stolen one of the pills of immortality, was transformed into a three-legged toad and transported to the surface of the moon, where she may be seen in outline today.

In the other version Heng O is the wife of Shen I, the Divine Archer, who, for special services to Chin Mu, the Golden Mother of the Tortoise, was awarded one of the same magic pills. This he carefully hid, but it gave forth such a delightful odor and radiant light that Heng O was drawn to it. She swallowed the pill and immediately found herself capable of levitation. In fact, she floated all the way to the moon before coming to rest. Here, while sitting under a cinnamon tree, she was subject to a great pain and in a violent fit of coughing spat out the coating of the pill. This was immediately transformed into a rabbit as white as pure jade. He may be seen in many jade carvings of this legend, standing under a cinnamon tree busily mixing the pills of immortality with a large mortar and pestle.

Needless to say, the chief ingredient of these pills was $CaMg^3$ $(SiO^3)^4$, or nephrite.

The Taoists might be said to have reached a peculiar impasse. While magicians and alchemists the world over had for thousands of years sought the philosopher's stone, the magic elixir of eternal life, the Taoists believed they possessed it in the form of jade. All they lacked was the exact knowledge of how to use it: the proportions to be consumed, the quantity and kinds of other substances with which to be mixed, the auspicious conditions under which it was to be worn or taken. In their fanciful and colorful quest they departed far from the original intention of their founder, Lao-tse, who perhaps came closer than they to discovering the secrets of creation by being in quiet harmony with all nature. Undoubtedly they chose to overlook one remark he had made: "Do not wish to be rare like jade, or common like stone."

An obsession with longevity and immortality . . . Man carrying the magic peach of eternal life. Sea-green jadeite with brown traces. H: 10″. 19th or 20th century. Courtesy M. H. De Young Memorial Museum, San Francisco, California. Avery Brundage collection.

IV. BUDDHISM AND JADE

At the time the young Prince Siddhartha lived in India, about five hundred years before Christ, the Chinese art of jade carving was at least two thousand years old. With the possible exception of its still unknown beginnings, it was a native art, which had matured free from foreign influence. Yet when the young Prince rose from his vigil under the bodhi tree, enlightened and henceforth known as Gautama, the Lord Buddha, he set in motion a chain of events which were to affect profoundly this art of far Cathay. One might argue as to which was more pronounced, however, the influence of the alien Buddhism on Chinese jade carving or the importance accorded carved jade in Chinese Buddhism.

New Dimensions for an Art

Buddhism came to China about A.D. 67. For almost two hundred years it made little impress on either the Chinese nobility or the Chinese arts. But it spread rapidly through the mass of the Chinese people, who found that it enriched rather than replaced their former beliefs. As one scholar, Mou Tzŭ, expressed it, "Confucianism was the flower, but Buddhism is the fruit." Though some of the Buddhist beliefs, with their roots in Hinduism, were contrary to Chinese thought, the greater part of the new religion was particularly suited to China's religious and cultural tradition. And China, with its marvelous digestive powers, assimilated the rest, so that it was not long until Buddhism seemed almost natively Chinese.

The most evident changes effected by Buddhism in the art of jade carving concerned size and subject matter.

Prior to the advent of Buddhism, jade carvings were generally small. The dagger axes and scepters of Shang, among the largest pieces, were usually under 2 feet in length. The *Pi* rarely exceeded 10 inches in diameter; few *Ts'ung* were taller than 1 foot. It is doubtful whether anyone had attempted anything to compare in size with the huge jade Buddhas, which sometimes exceeded life size.

It is not possible to establish just when the first of these were carved. One jade Buddha, 4 feet 2 inches high, was *said* to have been presented to China's ruler by the King of Ceylon in A.D. 404, but either the date or the importation appears to be incorrect, for jade carving did not spread to Ceylon until much later. A green jade tablet 4 feet 8 inches high, on which twenty Buddhas were carved, was said to have been completed in A.D. 476. This piece has been displayed in the United States. There have been a number of other jade Buddhas of similar dimensions, a few of which now reside in museums and private collections in the United States and Europe. Most appear to have been carved sometime after A.D. 500.

Probably the largest, and certainly the most famous, is the "Jade Buddha" (*Yü Fo*), which at last report sat in the Mongol Throne

Room overlooking the Forbidden City of Peking. It depicts the Lord Buddha seated in meditation. From his lotus throne to the top of his head is over 5 feet; he measures 3 feet in breadth and is more than 1 foot thick. The carving is one of the mysteries of Chinese art. First, no one is sure that it is really jade, since no one has been allowed to examine it closely. Second, its total concept, particularly the painted features, is unmistakably Indian, not Chinese. It is reputed to have been sent to the Chinese Emperor Ch'ien Lung by the King of Cambodia in the eighteenth century.

The Pagoda

Another large form which came into China with Buddhism is the pagoda. Not only did it change the architectural face of China, but it was in time to appear in jade. Two unusual examples have been displayed in the United States.

One, a modern carving commissioned by John Wenti Chang, was exhibited at the Century of Progress Exhibition in Chicago in 1933 and the Golden Gate International Exposition in 1940. Nearly 2,000,000 working hours, and the talents of one hundred and fifty workmen, went into this finely detailed carving. It stood about 50 inches high, was 13 feet in diameter at its base, and weighed about 50 lbs.

The other is older, carved in 1710 during the reign of the Emperor K'ang Hsi, and among the many jades that came to the West following the looting of the Peking Summer Palace. Nine feet tall, this pagoda once sold for $75,000. It is now on display in the University of Oregon Museum. Ornamented with 72 bronze bells, the pagoda is so placed in the museum that when there is a breeze from the Pacific the bells tinkle softly.

Many of the largest concepts in jade which followed the example of Buddhism—the huge mountain masses, the great Mongol wine bowl, the chimes and screens—will be discussed in detail in later chapters. It was the purely Buddhist figures, necessary for temple worship, which originally expanded the dimensions of jade carving.

Buddhas, Lohans, and Bodhisattvas

All of the Buddhist deities became familiar subjects in jade. There was not one Buddha, but several: in addition to Shakyamuni, the Lord Buddha, there was Maitreya, the coming Buddha, yet to

When there is a breeze from the Pacific the bells tinkle softly . . . Jade pagoda, ornamented with bronze dragon heads and bells. Delicate green "moss-in-snow" nephrite. H: 9′. Carved in 1710, during the reign of the Emperor K'ang Hsi. Courtesy University of Oregon Museum. Winston Guest collection.

be reincarnated, also known as the Laughing Buddha, of great corpulence and pleasant demeanor; Ananda, who will follow him, usually shown as teaching; and the multitudinous Buddhas who preceded Shakyamuni.

Next come the Lohans, the semi-mythical followers of the Lord Buddha. These are eighteen in number, including two early Chinese Buddhist historical figures. Like the Taoist Immortals, each was best known for special attributes and magic powers.

By no means last, but perhaps, next to Shakyamuni himself, the most beloved by the Chinese people, are the Bodhisattvas. These are beings who reached the pinnacle of spiritual enlightenment

Lohan: Semi-mythical follower of the Lord Buddha . . . Opaque sea-green nephrite. H: 6″. W: 7½″. D: 3″. Ming Dynasty. Courtesy William Rockhill Nelson Gallery of Art, Kansas City, Missouri.

but instead of seeking the final release chose to aid those still struggling through life's great experience. Best known, and the special favorite of the Chinese people, is the hauntingly beautiful Kuan Yin, the Jade Goddess, the Bodhisattva of Mercy.

Kuan Yin

Kuan Yin was a Buddhist who, through great love and sacrifice during life, had earned the right to enter Nirvana after death. But, standing before the gates of Paradise, she heard a cry of anguish from the earth below. Turning back to earth, she renounced her reward of bliss eternal but in its place found immortality in the hearts of the suffering.

From early Ch'ing times to the present, many thousands of statues of Kuan Yin have been carved in jade. The Maternal Goddess, the Protectress of Children, the Observer of All Sounds, Kuan Yin is a favorite figure in domestic shrines. As well, her image is carved on small jades which Chinese women offer faithfully at the temples dedicated to her.

She is usually depicted standing tall and slender, a figure of infinite grace. Her features, gently composed, convey the sublime selflessness and compassion that have made her the favorite of all deities.

Buddhist Symbols

This by no means covers the entire range of Chinese gods and goddesses immortalized in jade. There are dozens of other Buddhist figures, as well as many non-Buddhist gods of the door, hearth, walls and ditches, happiness, wealth, Heaven and Hell, the sea, the mountains and streams. More important than many of these lesser figures, however, are a few of the distinctly Buddhist symbols which in time became standard in non-Buddhist jade carvings.

The lotus, one of the oldest and most sacred Hindu symbols, was another of Buddhism's decorative gifts to the Chinese. Growing out of the mud of life, it nevertheless is not defiled, just as the Buddha was born into the world but rose above it. The lotus is sometimes the subject of individual jade carvings but more often a less conspicuous motif. Often it serves as a throne for carved Buddhas; frequently a god or goddess is portrayed holding it.

Other Buddhist symbols include prayer wheels, the swastika, the mystic knot, the conch shell, the peach, and the fly whisk.

Wheel enveloped in flames

Lotus flower

Conch shell

Vase

State umbrella

Pair of fish

Canopy

Endless knot

Eight Buddhist Emblems

Stone of an Enlarged Heaven

In addition to temple and household images of the deities, some of the other objects made of jade and utilized in Buddhist worship include:

The Buddhist rosary; prayer wheels; incense burners (some of the most beautiful as well as some of the most gaudily elaborate examples of the art); bowls; urns; ritual stands; candlesticks; tablets of the Buddhist scriptures and sutras, bound in book form; altar furniture; bells; chimes; lamaistic scepters; carvings of the

Buddhism added many new forms to jade carving, as well as expanded its physical dimensions . . . Buddhist assemblage. This large loaf-shaped piece is carved on both sides with minor Buddhist divinities and devils set in high relief among cloud motifs. Grayish-white nephrite. H: 5″. L: 16½″. Ming Dynasty. Courtesy Walker Art Center, Minneapolis, Minnesota. T. B. Walker collection.

Buddhist heavens, as well as scenes depicting every major incident in the life of Gautama; pendants; calendars; wheels of the law; fans; flutes; and drums (no example of the latter survives).

As this partial list indicates, Buddhism added many new forms to jade carving, as well as expanding its physical dimensions. However, jade's use in Buddhism was not entirely physical, for the Chinese did not discard their beliefs regarding jade when they became Buddhists, but rather found additional opportunities for confirming or expressing them. Thus in Buddhism, as in nature worship and ancestor worship, jade was "Heaven's stone" and treated accordingly. The early beliefs of the Chinese, as expressed in the Yang-Yin cosmology of the Taoists, were completely compatible with Buddhist beliefs about the nature of the universe—so much so that one suspects an origin common to both.

Zen

The form of Buddhism which most nearly approaches the earliest Chinese attitude toward jade, however, is Zen Buddhism, with its stress on the intuitive perception of nature. Zen, introduced into China by the monk Bodhidharma in about the first half of the sixth century, appears to have had no influence on jade carving itself. Yet jade was not unappreciated by the Zen monks.

Sometimes the advanced disciple was given a small piece of nephrite by his Zen master and told to meditate upon it. As he sat quietly concentrating upon the stone the disciple could: think about the carving; reminisce in detail on all he had ever heard or seen concerning jade; or, as his master intended, he could clear his mind of all preconceptions and see into the real nature of the stone, becoming one with it.

Thus jade, long believed to be the bridge between this world and the next, was actually used as a path to realization of the god-nature within man.

A modern Yoga master, Sri Subramuniya, who received his training in Ceylon, noted spontaneously, upon being handed a piece of carved nephrite: "This is very unusual. It has the same vibration as the first stage of Samadhi, when one experiences the Self or God flowing through all form." Samadhi is the highest state of contemplative experience in Hindu and Buddhist religions. It has been defined as the direct, instantaneous perception of reality.

Another curious bit of lore: Most Eastern religions state that when a man dies his spirit leaves the body through the crown of the head. The Hindus call this spot the *brahma sutra,* or "door of mystery." Chinese Buddhists call it the *Yü Men,* the Jade Gate.

Myth? Superstition? Or does jade, by its very nature, transcend the limitations of this world? That is one of the great secrets residing in the heart of this stone.

V. CHRISTIANITY, MOHAMMEDANISM, AND JADE

During the seventh century A.D., both Nestorian Christianity and Mohammedanism were introduced into China. Christianity soon adopted jade as a material for many of its accessories of worship, including crucifixes, rosaries, altar ornaments, and statuary. Mohammedanism restricted its use of jade to vessels of absolution. Yet the latter, rather than the former, made the most important contributions to jade carving.

The Fateful Decree

Christianity's part in the story of jade would undoubtedly have been greater had it not been for a papal decree made in the early eighteenth century.

When K'ang Hsi ascended the throne in 1662 the prospects for a Christian China were particularly bright. The Jesuits had great influence over the Manchu line; they had built a cathedral near the Palace at Peking, had supplied tutors for the royal family, and much of China had begun to embrace the new religion. By 1700 China was almost a part of Europe.

Then came talk of a papal bull (not actually issued until 1742) declaring that a Chinese, in order to become a Christian, must first renounce his former beliefs and institutions, including ancestor worship, Confucianism, and the Chinese Heaven. All of China revolted in the first large persecution of Christians in that country. Cruel edicts against all Christians, Chinese and foreign, were issued by the Emperor Yung Chêng during his reign (1723–35). The opportunity for Western civilization to incorporate China peacefully was lost and has never returned. Most of the Christian articles of worship in jade were either destroyed or carved into new forms. For at least six centuries these objects had provided an important medium for the jade craftsman. Today only a few are still in existence.

Monopoly Without Change

Mohammedanism fared better. For while the Moslems restricted their use of jade to the absolution vessels used prior to prayer, they took over almost completely the jade industry itself.

They were no strangers to jade. The area in which nephrite was mined was Moslem territory, the cities and villages along the great trade route were predominantly Moslem, and the men who transported the rough stone into China were Moslems (only Moslems could safely pass the Moslem pirates along the route).

In 1946 an American jade expert attended the funeral of a well-known Hong Kong jade merchant. To his surprise, he discovered that nearly all of the jade merchants of Shanghai were there, in Moslem dress.

Before the advent of the Communist government, out of three hundred million Chinese, over thirty million were Moslems. The great majority of merchants, lapidaries, carvers, and workers in jade were Chinese Moslems. Yet, though they completely dominated every phase of jade carving, they held the ancient art to its traditional courses, adding few if any of their own symbols and forms.

Thus jade, the stone of immortality, played its part in all of China's major religions and philosophies. For some it was the core of their worship; for others, the way to eternal life; and still for others, a microcosm of both earth and Heaven, reflecting the virtues of each.

CHAPTER FIVE

THE JADE DYNASTIES

Magnificent Ch'ien Lung vase, based on an ancient
bronze form. The honest inscription on the bottom
reads: "Ch'ien Lung, Antique Style." Green
nephrite. H: 11½". W: 7". Courtesy M. H. De
Young Memorial Museum, San Francisco, California.
Avery Brundage collection.

From the large cup of jade
Fragrant spirits down flow
Self possession and ease
Did our prince ever show
Could there but on him descend
Rank and blessing without end.

Like mace of jade pure, clear and strong,
What majesty and grace belong
To those your helpers true!
The hope of all their praise all sing,
Through them, O courteous, happy King,
The nations' guide are you.

The vessels formed of metal and jade
By graver's tool are still more precious made:
With grace their worth is thus combined.
Increasing were the labors of our King;
East, West, North, South, his laws and rules
shall bring
The reverent homage of each mind.

Selections from "The Book of Odes" (*Shih Ching*)
probably written between 800 and 600 B.C.

If a stone could speak, what a story jade would tell!

It might begin by describing the millions of years man treats so lightly, in only a few words—tremendous heat, unbelievable pressure and friction, slow interaction of water and minerals—its own evolution into jade stone.

It might speak next of the evolution of man. Of the primitive, perhaps even savage, first man who discovered and used jade, and of how he set a pattern that all men would follow—seeing in the stone that which he most needed and desired. For him it was toughness and strength. For others it would be beauty, virtue, noble thought, usefulness, decoration, a path to the Divine.

The cast of characters would be large: concubines and kings, mystics and murderers, scholars, scoundrels, gentlewomen and saints, beauties, villains, heroes, gods, to name only a few. The range of emotions would be great: for there were men who waged war for jade and women who loved for it, men to whom its possession meant power and still others to whom it brought access to the secrets of the universe.

Then, perhaps, it would speak of the evolution of an art, its carving. This too would be a part of the story of man's evolution, inseparable from it, for all the forces which directed and affected man went into his carving of this stone. The addition of a single line, a new motif in decoration, the disappearance of a form (and hence a use) might indicate vast changes in a whole culture. A foreign conqueror, for example, or a burst of great creativity, or a mood of longing for the past.

There would be no myths in such an account, though man probably would not believe everything the stone told. There would be no long gaps in time, as there are in our story, no missing years. We would not have to search the other art forms to determine styles, as is often necessary now because of our lack of dated objects. If jade could speak we would learn a great deal more about the stone of Heaven, but even more important, we would better understand man.

Yet even in the little we know we can catch glimpses of the fantastic history in which jade, though a silent witness, played such a dynamic part. We can observe how some of the stylistic changes in the art reflected the times and tempo of China and its people. And we can at least come closer to understanding how jade remained a constant in the midst of constant change.

NEOLITHIC ERA: ? TO 1766 B.C.

The Missing Years

These are the missing years, when man first discovered and carved jade, initiating the evolution of one of China's finest arts. From these countless centuries comes a wealth of myth, poetry, and legend, but unfortunately very little carved jade. Some authorities, questioning the dating of even those few objects attributed to the neolithic era, say none.

Alfred Salmony, in his *Carved Jade of Ancient China,* gives only

NEOLITHIC PERIOD: Statue of a bird, possibly an idol. Green nephrite. H: 4⅛″. L: 5½″. W: 2¾″. Tentatively dated 2nd or 3rd millennium B.C. Courtesy William Rockhill Nelson Gallery of Art, Kansas City, Missouri.

three illustrations of nephrite for this prehistoric time. One, the figure of a bird, possibly an idol, of green nephrite, in full-round, is captioned "Neolithic period." The others, a fish of greenish jade, carved on both sides and badly decomposed, and a human statuette two inches high, also of greenish jade, bear the safer designation "Neolithic *style*." All three are primitively naturalistic.

But, even with the addition of the supposedly neolithic finds of Dr. J. G. Andersson, which include several large finely wrought heads of jade in bronze hefts and settings and several flat rings, there are not enough examples available to establish a definite neolithic style in jade, nor is there enough real evidence to label these carvings definitely as neolithic.

Surely jade was carved during these years. Why has so little been discovered?

Perhaps the answer lies in the Chinese accounts of this "legendary" period.

Legendary or Historical?

We should realize that *we* are the ones who call this period legendary; the Chinese have always considered it historical. Just as their records spoke of the Chou and Shang dynasties and Western scholars doubted their existence until recent excavations, so time may again prove the Chinese annals correct, particularly in regard to the legendary Hsia Dynasty, which is said to have preceded the Shang civilization.

Chinese legends tell of a Great Deluge, similar to that mentioned in the Old Testament, which lasted twelve years and destroyed a good portion of populated China. The Emperor Yü, said to have founded the Hsia Dynasty in 1994 B.C. and credited with having the first bronze vessels cast, is also known as the Great Engineer Yü. Yü diverted the flood by methods similar to those used in modern irrigation, thus saving a large portion of the land and becoming a folk hero of Chinese farmers.

Remembering that most of the inhabitants of early China probably lived near the Yellow River and were subject to the frequent ravages of its waters, we may have a very logical explanation for the absence of early jades and bronzes.

That jade passed through a neolithic style is unquestionable. That the gradual refinement of the art required many centuries is undisputed. As evidence, we have the marvelous jades of Shang.

SHANG DYNASTY: 1766 or 1550 B.C.–1122 or 1050 B.C.

A Fantastic Grandeur

The Shang jades are fantastic. As one author expressed it, they "display a grandeur that is independent of their size." They were the product of a highly civilized people, and they reflect it.

We have mentioned most of these jades in previous chapters: the thin representational weapons, daggers, axheads, and knives; the six ritual forms, including the best-known *Pi* and *Ts'ung;* small animal figurines, of both actual and mythological beasts; the tomb

SHANG DYNASTY: Ceremonial dagger-ax, the handle bronze, the blade light green nephrite. L: 10¾". Courtesy Seattle Art Museum, Seattle, Washington. Thomas D. Stimson collection.

SHANG DYNASTY: Bird.
Grayish-yellow nephrite
with dark mottling. H: 2¼″.
L: 1¾″. W: 1⅛″. Courtesy
William Rockhill Nelson
Gallery of Art, Kansas City,
Missouri.

jades, including the nine body jades; and other accessories of early nature worship.

Alfred Salmony has noted, "The repertory of Shang art is limited to relatively few forms and few renderings of each motif." But these few forms, with their rigid stylization, show that the craftsmen had developed an amazing skill in their art.

Take the animals. Unlike the naturalistic creatures we cautiously label neolithic, the Shang animals are usually highly stylized. Most of their features conform to a set formula. Some, particularly the birds, are minutely detailed. Probably few if any of the designs and motifs were purely decorative. There is every indication that their symbolism was still understood by the craftsman and was a vital factor in his creation.

Compared to those of a later date, the Shang jades are fairly plain. In our modern sense of color, they are almost colorless, most

SHANG DYNASTY: Ornament, mask. Its curved back suggests either a special use or recutting from an earlier piece. Cream-colored nephrite. H: 1¼″. Courtesy Fogg Art Museum, Harvard University, Cambridge, Massachusetts. Grenville L. Winthrop collection.

of them being various shades of brown or gray. Rather than detracting from our appreciation, however, these factors make us all the more conscious of the stone itself and the quality of its carving.

And the carving is surprisingly consistent in quality: nearly always superb. This is evident even in pieces which have undergone chemical alteration and are much calcined by long contact with the earth. In numerous Shang pieces we discover early attempts at true relief carving, an indication of one of the coming directions of the art.

All of these elements combine to indicate a long, established tradition of jade carving, which may have begun, as several have surmised, well before 3000 B.C.

CHOU DYNASTY: 1122 or 1050 B.C.–256 B.C.

When the Chou rulers overthrew the Shang, they issued proclamations explaining their divine right to rule. One read: "Chou is an old people but its charge is new." There being little distinction between Shang jades and those of early Chou, their new charge did not reflect itself in jade until around 950 B.C.

But about this time jade carving and Chinese art in general

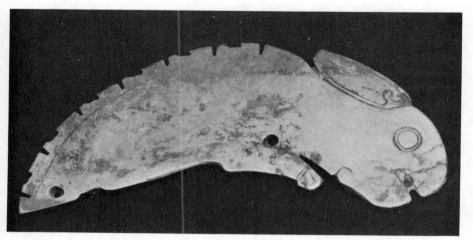

SHANG DYNASTY: Rabbit. Cream-colored nephrite with traces of blue. L: 4¾".
Courtesy Fogg Art Museum, Harvard University, Cambridge, Massachusetts.
Grenville L. Winthrop collection.

CHOU DYNASTY: Belt hook in the form of a praying mantis. A simplified and elongated motif. Grayish-tan nephrite flecked with reddish brown. L: 3⅜". Courtesy William Rockhill Nelson Gallery of Art, Kansas City, Missouri.

underwent a major shift of focus. Largely because of the expansion of the borders of China and the inclusion of a larger mass of people, many old forms fell into disuse or were dropped, while new forms appeared. There was a trend toward simplification in design. Several motifs, such as the dragon, the most popular symbol of the period, were both simplified and elongated. It was probably during this same time that the great quantity of jade used in dressing the corpse was no longer deemed necessary, with a subsequent loss of forms and designs. Most of the funerary jades were now identical to those used in daily life, as in the case of ornaments.

The trend did not last. During the latter days of the dynasty, about 600 B.C., the style again shifted, to extreme elaboration. The introduction of iron tools, making possible a greater command of the material, hence more complicated patterns, was probably one factor. (We shall consider this in more detail in Chapter Eight, on the carving of jade.) The most important, however, also occurring in the bronzes of this period, was a desire to make use of the materials' decorative qualities, a moving away from ritual austerity.

"The main characteristic of the new artistic language . . ." wrote Alfred Salmony, "is complete formalism. Now, every detail of the

LATE CHOU DYNASTY: Tiger-like animal. During the latter days of the dynasty the style again shifted to extreme elaboration. Mottled nephrite. H: 1". L: 2 3/16". T: 3/16". Courtesy Art Institute of Chicago, Chicago, Illinois. Edward and Louise B. Sonnenschein collection.

composition becomes transformed geometrically, frequently to such an extent that the representation is unrecognizable. Never before in Chinese art was reality transformed to such an extent . . . At times a recognizable ornament, supposedly of symbolic meaning, is surrounded by so many geometric patterns that it is nearly absorbed . . ."

This too had its Yang and Yin: while the ritual meaning of the traditional symbols was often lost, the craftsmen had a new freedom in their carving, they could now begin exploring the potentialities of the stone, both in decoration and use.

Plate 10 Animal carving. An exceptionally fine example of the jade artistry of the Sung Dynasty period. Nephrite. H: 3½″. L: 5″. Courtesy M. H. De Young Memorial Museum, San Francisco, California. Avery Brundage collection.

For example, the simple, usually unadorned *Pi* disk of Shang times was now often covered with all manner of design, including complicated scrollwork and elongated animals, sometimes running over the rim of the disk. While the Emperor still used the *Pi* in ritual worship, others in the court were now wearing miniature *Pi's*, connected with metal wire, as brooches.

It was a period of technical refinement. Treatment of the surface of jade indicates an interest in the display of light and shade. Oblique cutting was introduced, consisting of sloping bands following the contours, often repeated on the other side of the slope. While Shang animals were usually carved in irregular outlines, the animals of Chou appeared in formalized motifs, often conveyed in simple silhouettes or in high relief. The crisscross pattern made its first appearance, as did plant designs. Motifs which had previously been singly arranged in a bi-lateral symmetrical pattern were replaced by a continuous over-all scheme. There was often a rhythmic grace to the whole piece, a playful inventiveness apparent in even the smallest objects.

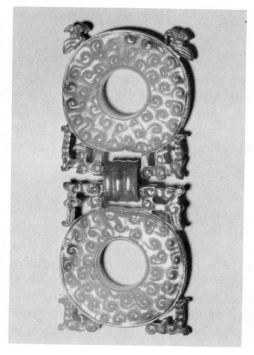

LATE CHOU DYNASTY: Winged disks, carved from a single piece of green nephrite. L: 2¾". W: 1¼". Courtesy Fogg Art Museum, Harvard University, Cambridge, Massachusetts. Grenville L. Winthrop collection.

LATE CHOU DYNASTY: Female figures, part of a large necklace. Light green and brown nephrite. H: 3¼". Courtesy Freer Gallery of Art, Washington. D.C.

Jade carving was undergoing gradual change from a naturalistic to a more civilized art, with attendant losses and gains. One could feel, in looking at many of these pieces, that jade was just another material to be decorated and carved, however skillfully; that the craftsmen had forgotten temporarily its legendary divine origin. In reality, however, they were just exploring another facet of its complex personality.

Girdle Jades

In addition to the prescribed ritual jades still in use, the nobility now used jade for numerous articles of adornment. Most common was the use of flat pendants (*p'ei yü*), which members of the Chou nobility hung from their belts. These "girdle jades," usually cut in the forms of animals, such as dragons, tigers, and fishes, were chosen for their resonance. When their wearer walked, the jades, striking against each other, made musical sounds. Sometimes they were so picked that each jade would sound a different note

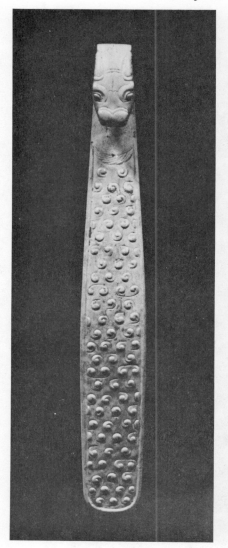 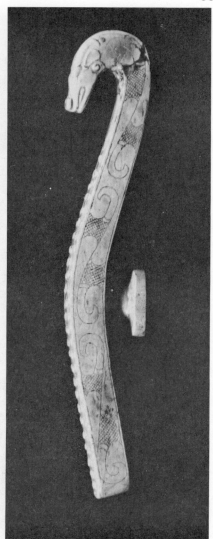

CHOU DYNASTY: Garment hook, top view and side view. Pale cream nephrite. L: 5¼″. W: 5/16″. T: 3/16″. Courtesy Freer Gallery of Art, Washington, D.C.

Plate 11 A 20th-century carving in jadeite. Note how the artist utilizes the red crust or rind as a part of the finished piece. H: 6″. W: 4″. Courtesy M. H. De Young Memorial Museum, San Francisco, California. Avery Brundage collection.

in the Chinese scale. These sounds were said to evoke thoughts of friendship and the desire to please. The Chinese maiden, lying sleepless in the moon-filled night, could recognize the arrival of her lover by the music of his jades.

Other items of personal adornment in Chou times included thumb rings, buckles, belt hooks, scabbard and girdle clasps, beads, symbols of rank, necklaces, and combs. Jade was also used for knife hilts, knot openers, ornaments of chariots and furniture, small statuettes, and inscribed seals.

The Message of Jade

These were times when jade still conveyed Heaven's will to man.

One Chou general was too pompous from his repeated military successes to listen. On the eve of a great battle a spirit appeared to him in a dream, instructing him to wear a cap of deerskin trimmed with jade if he wished to remain undefeated. The general ignored the omen; his tactics went awry, his troops were slain, and the general himself surrendered in defeat.

But to the young, jade spoke only one message: Love.

"Though you . . . are as fair as jade / Do not let the news of you be as rare as gold or jade, / Keeping your thoughts far away," sighs one young maiden in "The Book of Odes," believed to have been compiled during early Chou times. Another's more rapturous song also appears in this volume, superbly translated by Arthur Waley:

> There in the oozy ground by the Fên
> I was plucking the sorrel;
> There came a gentleman
> Lovely beyond compare,
> Lovely beyond compare,
> More beautiful than any that ride
> With the duke in his coach.
>
> There on a stretch by the Fên
> I was plucking mulberry leaves;
> There came a gentleman
> Lovely as the glint of jade,
> Lovely as the glint of jade,
> More splendid than any that attend
> The duke in his coach.

There in the bend of the Fên
I was plucking water-plantain;
There came a gentleman
Lovely as jade,
Lovely as jade,
More splendid than any that escort
The duke in his coach.

Yü (or jade) was by this time a synonym for beauty, an adjective for perfection. The Chinese were unsparing in their use of the word, often applying it in surprising ways. Goette notes some of them in his *Jade Lore:* jade tank (the kidneys), jade stalk (the penis), jade tower (the shoulders), ice jade (son-in-law), jade woman (wife), jade girl (daughter); "jade and stone will perish together" (punishment for good and bad alike); "she has transferred the jade lute to the other arm" (a widow has re-married); "the jade hill will fall" (our honored guest is dead drunk).

The First Vessels

A significant event in the carving of jade occurred during the latter part of the Chou Dynasty. For the first time, to our knowledge, vessels were carved in jade.

Numerous vessels were in use in Shang times, but to date none of jade has come to light, only a number of small jade plaques which were attached to vessels of other materials.

While most scholars agree that simple cups and bowls were carved in jade late in the Chou Dynasty, there is one question on which there is practically no agreement, and that is: When were the ritual vessels of bronze first reproduced in jade?

Berthold Laufer, in his pioneer work, *Jade: A Study in Chinese Archeology,* published in 1912, stated emphatically that sacrificial vessels of jade, resembling the bronze ritual vessels in shape and decoration, were in use in Chou times. Laufer based his opinion on what has since been proved, by S. Howard Hansford and others, to be an erroneous translation of a text of dubious authenticity. Even its illustrations were fraudulent, though of course Laufer was unaware of this.

Alfred Salmony did not venture an opinion, though he does ascribe cups and caskets to this period, supported by illustrations of objects excavated from Eastern Chou tombs.

LATE CHOU DYNASTY: Greenish-white nephrite cup with bronze cover, three low legs, and a ring handle, based on an ancient bronze form. Though most jade scholars disagree as to when the ritual bronze vessels were first reproduced in jade, there is general agreement that this cup and the one on page 140 were products of the late Chou Dynasty. H: 2¾″. D: 4¼″. Courtesy Fogg Art Museum, Harvard University, Cambridge, Massachusetts. Grenville L. Winthrop collection.

Hansford believes that the failure of such objects to appear during the last thirty-five years, "when so many remains of ancient China have been dug from her soil, suggests that jade vessels were not made during the Chou period, apart from the small, and relatively simple, pieces produced at the end of the dynasty."

He discredits the possibility that such objects were produced earlier than this, stating that in his opinion "jade vessels, even of this relatively simple kind, were not made before the use of rotary tools was well established. It would, I believe, be impossible to dig out the interior of a block of nephrite with a 'knife' held in the craftsman's hand."

The use of rotary tools in China is generally believed to have

Plate 12 Delicate flower maiden statuettes. H: 8″. W: 5″. Author's Collection.

occurred sometime after 500 B.C., when iron first came into use in tools of the jade craft.

Were the ritual sacrificial vessels copied in jade during the Chou Dynasty?

If there is a final answer, it rests with some future archaeologist. We shall treat these jades in more detail when we come to the Sung Dynasty, where we can not only place them with assurance but can also examine this phase of the art in its maturity.

CH'IN DYNASTY: 255–206 B.C.

A Most Hated Man

There is no more hated Emperor in the history of China than Shih Huang Ti, who ruled during the Ch'in Dynasty. Under his hand the weak feudal states of China were united into a strong empire. By his command the Great Wall of China was built. At his order China's most famous jade was carved. But he is re-membered by the Chinese as a destroyer. Wanting all future peo-ple to think history began with him, believing that literature could be given fresh stimulus only if begun anew, he ordered all existing books destroyed, including priceless literary and historical treasures. Fearful of any reminder of more peaceful times, he ordered the

HAN DYNASTY: Buckle with sprinting antelope. Cream-colored nephrite with brown markings. L: 2⅞". Fogg Art Museum, Harvard University, Cambridge, Massachusetts. Grenville L. Winthrop collection.

LATE CHOU DYNASTY: Light green and brown nephrite cup with the same general characteristics as the lacquers of the period. Side view. H: 1¾". L: 5¼". D: 4⅛". Courtesy Freer Gallery of Art, Washington, D.C.

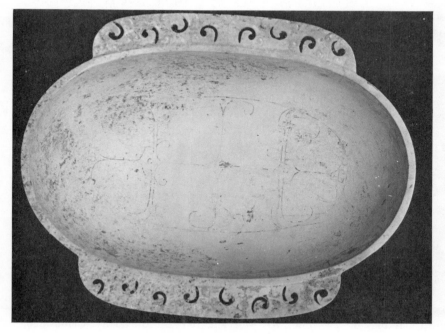

Inside view of the above.

destruction of many jades. Girdle pendants were replaced with swords.

The Emperor was not so foolish as to destroy all jades, however. Ironically, and possibly in partial compensation for his jade edict, he ordered the carving of the most famous jade in Chinese history, the Imperial Seal, which "transmits the state" and is the subject of the next chapter.

The people did not take kindly to this man who called himself the *First* Emperor of China. But you can't say he wasn't forewarned. Early in his reign a meteorite fell to earth with what was believed to be an inscription carved upon it prophesying the division of his empire. As confirmation that his days were few, a jade circlet he had tossed into the Yangtze River for sacrifice was mysteriously returned to him. Shortly after Shih Huang Ti's death in 210 B.C., the Ch'in Dynasty fell. The Emperor's tomb was ransacked, his relatives slain. It is said that the fire to which the people consigned his Palace smoldered for three months.

HAN DYNASTY: A.D. 206–220

It might be an exaggeration to claim that Confucius was responsible for the governmental and literary renaissance in the Han Dynasty, and Lao-tse for the renaissance in art. But only a slight one. For Confucianism and Taoism absorbed and to a great extent superseded the elements of primitive nature worship, to become the dominant philosophic and religious influences during the entire Han Dynasty.

Confucius' contribution to jade, as already noted, lay mainly in his translation of the ancient texts which linked jade inseparably to state religious rites. As previously mentioned, the Taoism of Lao-tse restored mystic and supernatural qualities to jade, surrounding it with a host of legends and myths, spirits and demons, immortal properties and motifs.

In style, a greater naturalism, which took into account the inherent attributes of the stone, gradually replaced the formalism of Chou. There were sculptural full-rounds, larger than heretofore, fine carvings of horses, bears, and other animals. Many motifs were simplified, particularly the human figure. Ornamental addition no longer interrupted the outlines of the subject. The Han jades testify decorative possibilities were not forgotten.

During this dynasty there was apparently increased interest in

Plate 13 Graduated bead necklaces and handbag ornament. Author's collection.

Plate 14 Jewelry. A many-colored jadeite bracelet and a ring with a perfect Imperial green cabochon. Author's collection.

the dead. Again jade could be divided into two main categories: practical and funerary. The Han clay tomb figures are well known today; many remarkable jade funerary statuettes also survive. These were larger than earlier human carvings, and often in full-round. The absence of a bore hole indicates they were not used as ornaments. There were jade mirrors as well, which, since they didn't reflect, must also have been solely for burial use.

In addition to the ornamental jade forms which survived Chou times, and the new Taoist forms, Han craftsmen also carved numerous interlinking friendship rings, animal charms, hair ornaments, clasps, bracelets, buckles and beads, and a jade lock which, when worn around the neck of a child, was believed to fasten him to the earth, locking him securely in his bodily form.

The fungus of immortality, sacred to the Taoists, was also frequently carved. It is possible that this branch-shaped growth was the prototype for the *Ju I*, the scepter-like jade which was given as a birthday and good-luck token in later dynasties and used ceremonially up to the time of the republic. And at least one text from this period refers to garments which consisted of jade plaques joined by gold thread like a coat of mail.

Another Han object of special interest was the tally. Carved most often in the sculptural figure of an animal, such as the tiger, the tally was cut in two parts, which were interlocking, one side rilievo, the other intaglio. The commander of the army would keep one half, his commander in the field the other; then one half would be sent with important messages, to establish their authenticity to the receiver.

HAN DYNASTY: Bear sitting on haunches. Funerary statuette of green nephrite. H: 1⅜". W: ½". Fogg Art Museum, Harvard University, Cambridge, Massachusetts. Grenville L. Winthrop collection.

HAN DYNASTY: Ritual Ts'ung. Gray nephrite. H: 12¾″. W: 3½″. Courtesy M. H. De Young Memorial Museum, San Francisco, California. Avery Brundage collection.

The Jade Coffin

The Han Dynasty Annals tell us that during the first century A.D. a curious event *was said* to have occurred, in which jade again acted as a Heaven-sent token.

A jade coffin mysteriously appeared in the hall of the Imperial Palace. It was so heavy the courtiers could not move it. When told of it, the Emperor realized it signified the end of his reign. Dressing in his official robes, he climbed into the coffin and lay down. The lid immediately snapped shut. He was buried the following day, his retainers discovering that the coffin could now be lifted without effort.

Stylistic Affinities

Though we are dealing with jade alone, the art of jade carving was a part of the great creative flow of all Chinese art. Usually when a stylistic change occurred in jade, it was at the same time occurring in other art forms, such as bronze and ceramics. The formalism of Chou, the renewed naturalism of Han—all of the arts of these times reflected such attitudes.

Jade's closest stylistic affinity is to bronze. But affinities are also manifested in pottery and porcelain. *The Praeger Encyclopedia of Art* makes the following interesting statement in its section on jade:

"The invention of porcelain was to no small degree due to attempts to obtain the resonance of jade in a material that was both more easily accessible and less hard to work." It further quotes the Châi Emperor's wish for porcelain to be made "as blue as the sky, as clear as a mirror, as thin as paper and as resonant as jade."

THREE KINGDOMS: A.D. 220–280
SIX DYNASTIES: A.D. 280–589
SUI DYNASTY: A.D. 589–618

Transition

For four hundred chaotic years kingdoms rose and fell like waves, leaving behind them little datable jade. It is possible that because of the great internal strife in China during this period hardly any jade was mined or imported. Most of the pieces we can attribute to these centuries are traditional and imitative of earlier periods.

For jade this must have been a transitional period, but the introduction and spread of Buddhism gave new spirit to the art, an impetus which, as previously mentioned, was to change its dimensions but not its meaning. It was to reach its apex during the T'ang Dynasty.

T'ANG DYNASTY: A.D. 618–907

Many forces went into making the T'ang Dynasty "the golden age of mature artistic production," as Alfred Salmony has labeled it.

There was the spiritual rejuvenation of Buddhism; the influence of Persian, Grecian, Indian, and Byzantine art forms; the rediscovery of China's artistic heritage.

But surely, equally important, these were luxurious times. Much nephrite must have been brought into China during this period, for at no previous time had jade been used so lavishly for personal adornment.

As is the wont with periods of opulence, there was a strong tendency toward overelaboration, the Chinese being a little too receptive to foreign styles in art. As if in balance, renewed interest in China's past caused the craftsmen to imitate many of the more severe ancient forms. Jade was still associated with cult usage; it was during the T'ang Dynasty that the edict forbidding inferior jades for funerary purposes was issued. Such an edict would have been meaningless unless there was a fairly large supply of the stone.

Yang Kuei-fei: China's Most Beautiful Woman

Chinese historians tell us that during China's long history there were two women whose beauty surpassed that of all the others combined.

Their names were Mei Fei and Yang Kuei-fei. Both lived during the T'ang Dynasty. Both were mistresses of the Emperor Ming Huang (also known as Hsüan Tsung). And, of course, they were bitter enemies.

SIX DYNASTIES: Sculptured group of boy and reclining elephant. Grayish-white nephrite with large patches of black and tan, patches of pinkish purple, and spots of light green. Satin-smooth surface. H: 5¾". L: 3⅜". Courtesy Freer Gallery of Art, Washington, D.C.

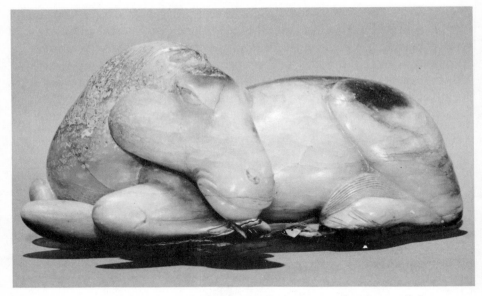

T'ANG DYNASTY: This carving of a sleeping horse is considered one of the
finest examples of the jade carver's art. Yellow and brown nephrite. H: 2⅜".
L: 5¼". Courtesy Art Institute of Chicago, Chicago, Illinois. Edward and
Louise B. Sonnenschein collection.

The Emperor met Mei Fei first and made her his concubine,
sure that no lovelier woman existed. But then he saw Yang Kuei-
fei, the betrothed of his son, the heir apparent.

Her skin, T'ang chroniclers tell us, was "as white and smooth as
jade," her features "as finely carved as jade," but her heart, to her
own undoing, was not as cool as jade.

The Emperor saw her, displaced Mei Fei, and made Yang Kuei-
fei his own.

Installed as his concubine, she became known as the Jade
Beauty, for it is said that she slept on a "jade bed," wore only jade
ornaments, and surrounded herself only with objects of jade.

From her robes hung a large variety of tasseled jades in the shape
of baskets, flowers, fruit, birds, bells, and animals. From her waist
hung a small jade cylinder which exuded the fragrance of crushed
blossoms. In her long black hair, knotted in the back, were two long
jade hairpins and two pierced white ornaments of jade. When wearing her festive headdress, there were dozens of additional jades:
small pendants in myriad forms and colors, elaborate earrings, and

a pair of festoons over a foot in length which hung from the head-dress.

On her arms were solid-jade bracelets; on her gently heaving chest, brooches of jade.

Yü was no less evident in her Imperial suite. Her furniture was ornamented with jade. On her dressing table were small jade bottles of perfume and feminine spices, a jade box for her jewelry, a jade tray, jade combs. She played upon a jade flute.

One night the Emperor dreamed that an evil spirit was attempting to steal Yang Kuei-fei's jades. But a second ghost appeared and devoured the thief. This ghost identified himself to the Emperor as a poor student who had killed himself after failing his examinations. Upon awakening, the Emperor had the student's body disinterred, gave it an honorable burial, and the ghost forever after protected the Imperial household.

Yang Kuei-fei's lover, the Emperor Ming Huang (we must be explicit, for she had two), also lived in a jade world. In addition to the Imperial jades custom required, the Emperor sat on a jade throne chair, secretly dallied with the dispossessed Mei Fei behind paper-thin jade screens, ate from jade dishes, encouraged his horse with a riding crop topped in jade, wrote on a jade plaque with a jade-handled brush. When nobles addressed him in court they held a jade tablet in front of their mouths so their breaths would not offend.

T'ANG DYNASTY: Comb top, carving depicts a man with a bow and arrow, hunting a rabbit. Greenish-yellow nephrite with areas of brown. L: 3⅜". Courtesy Seattle Art Museum, Seattle, Washington. Eugene Fuller collection.

Though the Jade Beauty was undoubtedly China's most exquisite woman, the Emperor was greedy and wanted to keep the second best too. Once, upon entering the Imperial bedchamber unannounced, Yang Kuei-fei noticed the jade hairpins of Mei Fei on the table. Pulling aside the window curtains, she discovered her rival, whereupon she threw her own jade jewelry to the floor and left in a rage.

On another occasion Yang Kuei-fei was herself visited unexpectedly. The young man was banished, but he returned to the capital some months later with an army, determined to kill the Emperor and rescue his beloved. The enraged Emperor demanded Yang Kuei-fei's death, and even the offer of all her precious jade ornaments to palace servants did not save her. In desperation the Jade Beauty hanged herself. But, as narrated in a long poem by Po Chu-i, this was not the end of her story; later, in a dream, Ming Huang

T'ANG DYNASTY: Camel biting his hump. Gray-green to brownish nephrite. H: 2¾". L: 4⅛". Courtesy Seattle Art Museum, Seattle, Washington. Eugene Fuller collection.

saw her knocking at the jade door of the Palace of Paradise.

All women of rank possessed at least some of the ornaments and accessories of jade ascribed to Yang Kuei-fei. By the T'ang Dynasty, we assume, although we have little evidence except the obvious availability of much jade, the ordinary people of China had begun to possess jade. It might be a single object—a fingering piece of polished but uncarved jade, a girdle ornament, or a pendant worn upon the person to ward off evil thoughts and desires. It was probably very cheap and of inferior quality. But it was jade, the stone of Heaven, and probably more appreciated as such than all the baubles of Yang Kuei-fei.

We might also say that by the time of the Jade Beauty jade was no longer considered an exclusively masculine stone. Certainly the lot of some women had improved since the following poem first appeared in the Chou Dynasty "Book of Odes":

> When a son is born,
> Let him sleep in a bed.
> Clothe him with fine dress and give him jades
> with which to play.
> How lordly is his cry!
> May he grow up to wear crimson
> And be the lord of clan and tribe.
>
> When a daughter is born,
> Let her sleep on the ground.
> Wrap her in common cloth,
> And give her broken tiles for playthings.
> May she have no faults, nor virtues of her own;
> May she well attend to food and wine,
> And bring no discredit to her parents.

(The poem, incidentally, is written in a style called Jade Verse.)

FIVE DYNASTIES: A.D. 907–960
SUNG DYNASTY: NORTHERN SUNG: A.D. 960–1125
SOUTHERN SUNG: A.D. 1125–1279

Interest in ancient forms and designs continued well into the Sung Dynasty, resulting in one of the finest periods in the history of the jade craft. The lavish ornamental jades of T'ang gave way to simpler, sturdier, less ornate pieces carved along ancient lines. Strength and restraint best describe the jades of this period,

SUNG DYNASTY: Cup. A fine example of the exceptional carving of the Sung period. Gray nephrite. H: 10″. W: 5″. Courtesy M. H. De Young Memorial Museum, San Francisco, California. Avery Brundage collection.

whether the object was a vase, a hatpin, or a reclining water buffalo.

Most important, during the Sung Dynasty, many archaic bronze ritual vessels were carved in jade. We say "carved" instead of "copied," for often these jade vessels were not exact reproductions but original creations based on antique forms. The craftsmen were not above "improving" upon the designs. In our own times, however, these same Sung jades have been much "copied." Many are outright forgeries.

Ritual Bronzes in Jade

Bronze forms, which date as far back as the Shang Dynasty and which may have been based on even earlier pottery forms, were used almost exclusively in court ceremonial worship. Only after they began appearing in jade were they used as well in household shrines, ancestral temples, and the like, often carved to note some particular auspicious occasion.

As the illustrations indicate, many of these jades were massive, with bold lines and strong planes. Yet it is to the credit of the craftsmen that these are not just bronze shapes appearing in another medium: the carver did not forsake the sensitivity and delicacy of

SUNG DYNASTY: Bowl, with dragons peering over the rim. Gray-green nephrite with mottled black and brown. H: 2″. L: 6½″. W: 4½″. Courtesy M. H. De Young Memorial Museum, San Francisco, California. Avery Brundage collection.

SUNG DYNASTY: Cup based on an archaic bronze form. Grayish-white nephrite with brown markings. H: 5¼″. Courtesy Walker Art Center, Minneapolis, Minnesota, T. B. Walker collection.

the smaller pendants and carvings but managed to transfer them into these new forms, in the interlinking chains connecting the lid to the body of a vase, in the angles of the carving, and especially in his choice of the perfect jade for a specified form.

Nor did he stop with the forms of the bronzes. In time, as he mastered these shapes, he moved on to plates so thin and delicately carved as to be almost transparent, and cups that in beauty rivaled the finest porcelain. It is said that one set of these cups, used by the Emperor, was so sensitive it would break upon contact with poison.

It was during this period that the first catalogues of jade collections were published. For many years these gave us our only knowledge of the still more ancient jades.

The Sung period in many ways resembled our present era. There was tremendous interest in ancient culture and a growing concern with meaning and philosophy. Zen Buddhism came to the fore, uniting the Taoist concept of being at one with the inner and basic forces of nature with the searching analytical Buddhist approach to life. Emphasis shifted from action to introspection. Art flourished. Painting and ceramics were at their height. But, as is true with every period, the Sung too had its Yin and Yang, its opposites. The wealth of the times contributed to smugness and a desire to retreat from the facts. Life was fat, too fat.

YÜAN DYNASTY: A.D. 1260–1368

Kublai and Genghis Khan

With the arrival of the hard-riding, ruthless Mongols, the artistically ideal Sung Dynasty collapsed. When Kublai Khan made himself the First Emperor of the Yüan Dynasty, the sleek, self-indulgent Sung era was finished. The conservative Confucians, seeing an opportunity to regain their lost power, united with the Mongols to suppress Taoism and Zen. The uncultured Mongols did not appreciate the subtleties of Chinese symbolism, the significance of form, or the cult of rare glazes. But they did understand *realism*, and during the Yüan period realism became the dominant force. It smothered many of the less sturdy art forms.

The progress of the jade craft was more checked than thwarted, however. In its favor, in one respect, was the fact that the Mongol rulers treasured jade vessels for serving food and wine.

SUNG DYNASTY: Vase in the form of a ceremonial bronze *tsun*. Brownish-white nephrite. The dragons and other motifs are in the style of the late Chou Dynasty. H: 7⅞″. Courtesy Walker Art Center, Minneapolis, Minnesota. T. B. Walker collection.

In 1318, Friar Oderic, a missionary, visited the palace of the Great Khan in Peking. He described what he saw there:

> In the midst of the palace is a large jar more than two paces in height, entirely formed of a certain precious stone called Merdacas [nephrite] and so fine that I was told its price exceeded the value of four great towns. It is all hooped round with gold, and in every corner thereof is a dragon represented as in the act to strike most fiercely, and this jar has also fringes of network of great pearls hanging therefrom, and these fringes are a span in breadth. Into this vessel drink is conveyed by certain conduits from the court of the palace, and beside it are many golden goblets from which those drink who list.

At the fall of the Mongols the jar disappeared. Then, in the eighteenth century, it (or a very similar vessel) was discovered in the kitchen of a Buddhist monastery, where, stripped of its gold and jewels, it was used for storing salted vegetables. The Emperor Ch'ien Lung bought it and composed an ode telling its story, which jade craftsmen carved on the inside of the bowl. It is 4 feet 4 inches in height, 3 feet 6 inches in diameter (Oderic's dimensions do not tally with modern measurements of this piece) and holds forty quarts of wine. We do not know whether the work was done during the Sung or Yüan period, but it does indicate one of the extremes of the art and the continuing high regard for jade.

Except for the expanded use of jade vessels and jade used for hilts of swords and knives (of Persian design), during the Yüan Dynasty jade for the most part held to its previous courses, less impressed by the Mongols than they by it.

When one of the descendants of Genghis Khan, Tamerlane (Timur the Lame), died in 1405 while preparing to reconquer China, his tomb was said to have been made inviolate with a huge slab of jade.

But the Mongols were to make their mark on jade, though indirectly. In about the sixteenth century they encouraged Chinese craftsmen to journey to India, where they established studios and taught the art. Some of the products of Indian carving were in time to come back into China as Imperial gifts. Indian jades differed from those of China in that they were inset with diamonds, gold, rubies, and emeralds; "an example of painting the lily that would hardly have commended itself to the Chinese jade carver, though the result is a fine glow of color," notes S. Howard Hansford.

MING DYNASTY: A.D. 1368–1644

With China freed from Mongol domination, it appeared that the creative renaissance of the Sung Dynasty might now blossom into full flower, but—except for the arts of cloisonné and jade—the movement failed. By the end of the fifteenth century the Confucians were again in charge of the government; formalism and controlled conformity ended most artistic progress.

A New Vigor

Yet, as is evidenced by the tomb of the Ming Emperor Wan-li (mentioned in detail in Chapter Two), the art of jade carving developed unabated. There is a new vigor in many of the carvings;

MING DYNASTY: Sculptured group of boy and horse. Note the vigor and robust strength of this carving. White and brown nephrite. H: 3½". L: 6". Courtesy M. H. De Young Memorial Museum, San Francisco, California. Avery Brundage collection.

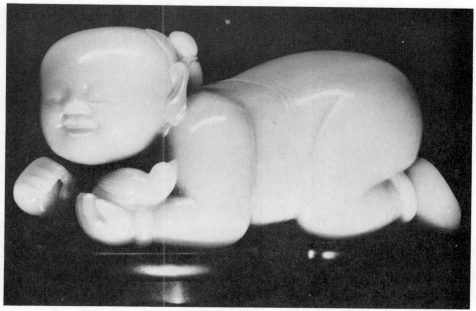

MING DYNASTY: Pillow in form of a nude boy holding a bird in his left hand. Greenish-white nephrite. H: 4½″. L: 8¾″. Walker Art Center, Minneapolis, Minnesota. T. B. Walker collection.

they are bold, dignified, baroque, with a robust strength. Lines are strong and sure. There are few, if any, new forms, but the jades are masterfully conceived and carved.

The scholar, as well as the court, was a ready market for jade. Jars to hold writing brushes, cups for water to mix with the ink, inscribed seals, paperweights, knives, brush holders, boxes which held the ink slabs, rulers, armrests—these, as well as small balls (fondling pieces) which the scholar rolled in his hand to keep his fingers supple for painting and fine calligraphy, were all among the products of the jade artist.

Snuff Bottles

During Ming times a considerable trade was conducted with the West. It was at this time that tobacco from the Americas became a vogue in Europe, both for smoking and for snuff. Authorities differ on the date tobacco first reached China; it would be reasonably safe to guess that it probably occurred between 1600 and

MING DYNASTY: Tablet topped with a resting water buffalo. One of a set of six animal tablets. Mottled pale green and tan nephrite, partly translucent. H: 6½″. W: 2½″. Courtesy Freer Gallery of Art, Washington, D.C.

1650. As in Europe, taking snuff quickly became the fashion. However, unlike his Western counterpart, the Chinese was most hygienic in his use of snuff. While the Westerner would pass his snuffbox to his friends, inviting them to take a pinch, the Chinese kept his snuff in a small bottle, which also contained a tiny wooden or ivory spoon. He would dip out the snuff with the spoon, then carefully place it on the thumbnail of the man to whom it had been offered.

Often these snuff bottles were carved from jade. Today they are highly valued by collectors, many of whom consider them one of the finest technical and artistic achievements of the jade art. Lilla S. Perry deals knowledgeably and well with the subject in her beautiful book, *Chinese Snuff Bottles: The Adventures and Studies of a Collector.* Most jade snuff bottles date from later periods than the Ming; their carving reached its artistic peak during the reign of Ch'ien Lung (1736–95).

Musical Instruments

Since resonance was one of the stone's most cherished qualities, the ear was not ignored by the artisans of jade. As early as the Shang Dynasty we find evidence of the use of jade in musical instruments. Archaeologists unearthed a jade string holder, apparently once attached to a lute-like instrument of more perishable material. Ancient texts claim that during the Han Dynasty flutes were made of jade. Many later finely-wrought examples survive, as do jade bells. It is the jade chimes, however, which dominate jade musical instruments.

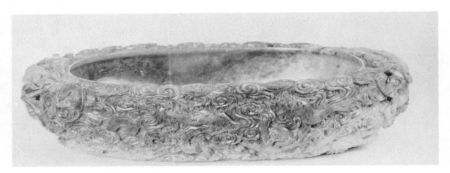

MING DYNASTY: Elaborately carved bowl of mottled gray nephrite. H: 2¼″.
L: 10″. W: 2¼″. Courtesy M. H. De Young Memorial Museum, San Francisco, California. Avery Brundage collection.

Texts credit the legendary Emperor Yao (2300 B.C.) with the poem which opens Chapter Four—"When I smite my jade musical stone . . ." This stone, the Ch'in, appears frequently in ancient texts, through all of the Chinese dynasties, but the only actual stones we possess date from the eighteenth century. That its use, when in jade, was restricted solely to the Emperor may account for its rarity today. If a prince or lesser official "used the jade Ch'in, they exceeded the limits of propriety."

Classical sources say there were originally sixteen small and one large Ch'in in a set. From the time of the Han Dynasty the number began increasing, stopping in the Ming Dynasty with twenty-four, then reverting to the original sixteen.

John Goette was the first non-Chinese- to measure and photograph a complete set when he catalogued the Imperial jades in the Forbidden City. At that time he knew of only three complete sets in Peking. Partial sets and single chimes are a little more frequent in the notable jade collections today. In form, the chimes resemble carpenters' squares.

MING DYNASTY: Tiger statue. Light green nephrite. H: 2⅜". L: 4¼". Courtesy Art Institute of Chicago, Chicago, Illinois. Edward and Louise B. Sonnenschein collection.

During sacrifices to Confucius the largest chime (the *T'ê Ch'ing*) is placed outside the main hall. One deep note is struck at the end of each verse of the rites, "to receive the sound." The smaller chimes (*Pien Ch'ing*) serve as accompaniment to the hymn. The stones are often carved, sometimes incised with gold figures and designs. They were hung from highly ornamented wooden racks and struck with a wooden mallet.

In sacrifices to the ancestors, the sound of the jade chimes, together with the flutes and drums, was said to draw the spirit of the respected departed to the place of the ceremony.

Chinese annals mention the jade flute of Han Hsuang-tze, whose tone caused flowers to grow and blossom miraculously. And Una-Pope Hennessey, in her *Early Chinese Jades*, tells the legend of the Emperor Kao-Tsu, who when playing his jade flute "conjured up mountains and rivers and groves and horses as in a mist—visions that vanished altogether as the notes of music died on the air."

Such is the resonance of jade.

CH'ING DYNASTY: A.D. 1644–1912

Two emperors made this dynasty the greatest in the history of jade carving: K'ang Hsi, who ruled from 1662 to 1722, and Ch'ien Lung, who ruled from A.D. 1736 to 1795.

K'ang Hsi

K'ang Hsi established studios for the carving of jade on the Palace grounds and brought there the finest jade craftsmen in the land, who turned out a large number of beautiful jades, of all sizes and descriptions, from the oldest jade forms to their own newly created designs. The Emperor himself spent many hours composing odes to be carved on the jades.

The most famous jade commissioned by K'ang Hsi is the carving of a white dragon-headed horse carrying the Books of Knowledge across the waves of the Yellow River. It was ordered carved in 1670 to complete a famous trilogy, which included a large reclining post-Han water buffalo and an unusual black jade horse of the T'ang period. All three now reside in the Fitzwilliam Museum, Cambridge, England.

During this dynasty nephrite from Chinese Turkestan was imported in greater quantity than ever before. The demand for

CH'ING DYNASTY (18th century): Ivory-white nephrite teapot, with rings on top. H: 6½". W: 5". Courtesy M. H. De Young Memorial Museum, San Francisco, California. Avery Brundage collection.

jade objects, from both the court and the public, was insatiable. Artistic patronage was common.

Ch'ien Lung

It was under the reign of Ch'ien Lung, however, that jade reached its peak of production and, many feel, excellence. Under an emperor who personally cherished small, delicately carved objects in pure-white jade, probably the largest jades ever carved were created in his Palace studios.

During his reign several exceptionally large nephrite blocks were brought into Peking. One, weighing 640 pounds, Ch'ien Lung ordered carved to represent a mountain landscape scene. On display today in the Walker Art Gallery in Minneapolis, Minnesota, it is the largest single jade piece in the United States, as well as one of the finest examples of the Ch'ien Lung period. On the majestic mountain of greenish-white jade are trees, streams, pavilions, and a bamboo grove where a group of fourth-century scholars is assembled. Ch'ien Lung wrote a special poem to be inscribed on the back of the mass.

An even larger jade mountain, estimated to weigh about seven tons, was carved from a single nephrite boulder sent to Emperor Ch'ien Lung by the governor of Chinese Turkestan in 1778. In

CH'ING DYNASTY (18th century): Covered bowls. The covers are of pure-white nephrite, the bowls of dark gray-green. H: 8″. D: 8″. Courtesy M. H. De Young Memorial Museum, San Francisco, California. Avery Brundage collection.

grayish-white jade, it stands seven feet tall, took ten years to carve, and depicts the heroic legendary Emperor Yü re-channeling the floodwaters.

There were other remarkable masses carved during this dynasty. Several give us a look into the activities of the Buddhist and Taoist heavens. Often the detail is as fine as on the smaller carvings. Mountain scenes appear, too, on smaller jades; sometimes a large pebble is so carved with one or two figures, the rough uncarved portion representing a rugged Chinese mountain.

But the craftsmen of Ch'ien Lung did not confine themselves to mountains. Indeed, one is almost tempted to say that if there was a conceivable use to which jade could be put, without sacrificing its natural characteristics, these artists discovered it.

CH'ING DYNASTY: The largest jade mountain mass in the United States. Both sides of this greenish-white nephrite boulder are carved to represent a mountain landscape, with human figures and pavilions. There are also two long poetic inscriptions by the Emperor Ch'ien Lung. Dated 1784. H: 22½″. L: 39⅜″. Walker Art Center, Minneapolis, Minnesota. T. B. Walker collection.

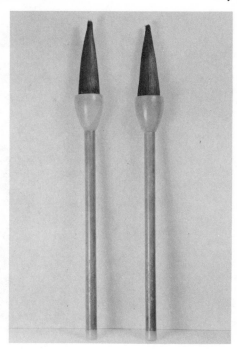

CH'ING DYNASTY (18th century):
Jade brushes. Gray-green nephrite
with gold inscriptions on the
handles. L of handles: 12".
Courtesy M. H. De Young
Memorial Museum, San Francisco,
California. Avery Brundage
collection.

Much emphasis was placed on the decorative aspects of the stone.

One of the more unusual uses of jade was for finger sheaths, often three or four inches long, usually of green or white jade, embossed with precious stones. These were worn both to protect the long nails and to indicate membership in the aristocracy, who did not have to labor with their hands.

Aladdin's Discovery

Among the extra tales which Richard Burton added to his translation of *The One Thousand and One Nights* was the story of Aladdin and his marvelous lamp. Originally a Chinese tale which made its way to Arabia, it contains within it still another use of jade.

> . . . Accordingly, Aladdin arose and descended into the souterrain, where he found the four halls, each containing four jars of gold and these he passed by, as the Maroccan had bidden him, with the utmost care and caution . . . Presently, descending the ladder he returned to the garden where he fell to gazing at the trees whereupon sat birds glorifying with loud voices their Great Creator. Now he had not observed them as he went in, but all these trees bare for fruitage

CH'ING DYNASTY (17th or 18th century): Brush holder. Dark green nephrite. H: 6¾". D: 8". Courtesy M. H. De Young Memorial Museum, San Francisco, California. Avery Brundage collection.

costly gems; moreover each had its own kind of growth and jewels of its peculiar sort; and these were of every colour, green and white; yellow, red and other such brilliant hues and the radiance flashing from these gems paled the rays of the sun in the forenoon sheen. Furthermore the size of each stone so far surpassed description that no King of the Kings of the world owned a single gem equal to the larger sort nor could boast of even one half the size of the smaller of them . . .

What Aladdin probably saw were Jade Trees, which stood several feet high and were fashioned out of wood or metal and ornamented with various colored jades and semi-precious stones, which represented rocks, leaves, flowers, and fruit.

The Ch'ien Lung craftsmen carved jade screens as detailed and as beautiful as a Chinese painting, as thin as one eighteenth of an inch, as wide as several feet; vessels whose lids are connected to the

CH'ING DYNASTY (18th century): A superb example of the art of the reign of Ch'ien Lung. Near-translucent plates of pure-white nephrite. H: 2". D: 7¼". Courtesy M. H. De Young Memorial Museum, San Francisco, California. Avery Brundage collection.

CH'ING DYNASTY (18th century): Ancient bronze form reproduced in light green nephrite. This piece may have been recut at a later date. H: 10". Courtesy M. H. De Young Memorial Museum, San Francisco, California. Avery Brundage collection.

body by long links, all carved from a single piece of jade; dishes, bowls, wine pots, censers, which must be seen and handled to convey their remarkable beauty. All manner of statues, vessels, and talismans. Articles of personal adornment, looking lost as they now rest in their museum cases, for you know their natural background was meant to be the skin of a lovely woman. All the ritual forms, some bearing the honest seal: CHOU DYNASTY PIECE. CH'IEN LUNG MADE. Small fondling pieces, usually carved from a single nephrite pebble. Jade furniture, tables, beds, even pillows. Books of jade.

As S. Howard Hansford said, "When we consider the extent to which jade clothing ornaments, accoutrements, and articles of luxury were in daily use by courtiers, scholars, and men and women of fashion in eighteenth-century Peking, it seems that there can have been few occasions when the precious mineral was out of sight in the palaces and stately homes of the capital."

Perhaps the very amount of activity in jade makes it unnecessary to note that the craftsmen occasionally went to new extremes in ornateness, some leaning more heavily on display of technical skill than on consideration of over-all effect. Yet many of the finest ornamental jades in our museums and private collections are products of the anonymous jade craftsmen under the tutelage of Ch'ien Lung.

CH'ING DYNASTY (18th century): Indian or Mogul jade. A very thin white nephrite bowl, decorated with gold, rubies, diamonds, and pearls. H: 2". D: 5". Courtesy M. H. De Young Memorial Museum, San Francisco, California. Avery Brundage collection.

The Jade Dynasties: Conclusion and Continuation

These were the dynasties of jade. The individual, in examining jades of these periods, may find himself drawn to a certain style or a certain form by personal preference. It may be a solemn symbolical *Pi* of milk-white jade, a spirited Sung horse of green jade, or a paper-thin grooved plate of Ch'ing.

But by all odds it will be a highly individual piece so immediately appealing, so responsive to the deepest feelings, that its style, its date of conception, its historical connotations are secondary to one's instant appreciation.

And that is one of the great qualities of fine jade—that it transcends not only space but also time. That it is a living, evocative stone, able to convey through the senses an awareness of that intuitive wholeness that lies beyond them, which is the experience of great art.

There are those who limit their appreciation of jade to pre-Han pieces. Others set the limits of their understanding at Ming. Still others believe nothing worthy in jade has been carved since Ch'ien Lung. It is natural and inevitable that each of us finds himself in greatest harmony with the arts of a certain period which perhaps best expresses our own emotions. But if we hold these lines firm and unyielding, refusing to listen when a piece of earlier or later vintage "speaks" to us, then we are denying ourselves access to the real beauty and magic of the stone, which is unfettered by pre-conceptions and time.

When the Emperor Ch'ien Lung stepped down from the throne in 1795, at the age of ninety-two, many of the Chinese arts entered into a period of decline. Jade is often included with them, but nothing could be farther from the truth. In 1784, during the reign of Ch'ien Lung, there was an occurrence which gave a new dimension and impetus to the art of jade carving, an event almost as momentous as the first discovery and use of nephrite by the Chinese.

But before telling this story and that of modern jade (from Ch'ien Lung to the present), we should like to backtrack for one short chapter to recount one of the most amazing stories in the lore of jade, the chronicle of the "precious jade of Ho," which for over two thousand years determined who would rule China.

CHAPTER SIX

THE PRECIOUS JADE OF HO

It is believed that if a sovereign be perfect in the observance of the rites of state, white jade will appear in the valley.

"The Book of Rites" (*Li Chi*)

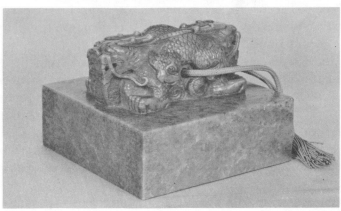

Imperial jade seal, similar in appearance to the seal of state discussed in this chapter. The above was carved following the death of the Emperor Hsien Feng and bears his posthumous title, "Wen Tsung Hsien Huang Ti." Carved of dark green nephrite. Dated January 1862. Courtesy Seattle Art Museum, Seattle, Washington.

From ancient times the Chinese Emperor spoke to Heaven through a piece of jade.

From about the third century B.C. another piece of jade functioned as Heaven's answer, becoming the divine symbol of the Emperor's right to rule. This was the precious jade of Ho, a jade seal said to "transmit the state." *The man who possessed it had the right to rule China.* For this reason the seal was to provide some of the most dramatic moments in Chinese history—as men fought, betrayed, stole, and died to obtain it—until well into our own century.

Legend tells us that Ho was a poor scholar who lived sometime before 500 B.C. While still a young man Ho saw a phoenix alight on a boulder. Familiar with his mythology, he decided the boulder was composed of exceptionally fine jade. His first and only thought was to present it to his ruler, which he did, with lavish praise of the stone's unusual merits. Court attendants didn't agree; they even doubted the stone was jade. For his impertinence Ho was punished with the severing of his left foot.

Ho was a patient man. And he believed in his jade. He waited, and when another sovereign mounted the throne he returned to the court, bearing his same gift. This time he had to be carried away, for loss of the right foot was decreed as his penalty for making a fraudulent offering.

To say the least, Ho was dedicated. One might even be tempted to say he was jade-mad. When the third ruler came into power Ho again repeated his journey. Only this time he was vindicated. The new Emperor recognized fine jade, and Ho was richly rewarded for his trials, tribulations, and losses.

Chinese annals give us two different accounts concerning the next development in the history of the precious jade of Ho. Though they are contradictory, we shall give both and let the reader choose his favorite.

The first story states that sometime after the beginning of his reign the King of Chao had the jade cut into a beautiful *Pi.* Hearing of its exceptional nature, the King of Ch'in offered fifteen cities in exchange for it. The King of Ch'in was not noted for his honesty, yet fifteen cities!

The King of Chao decided to take the gamble. With the jade he sent a wily prince, who promised to return with either the deeds to the cities or the jade.

Once in the court of the King of Ch'in, the Prince learned, through various intrigues, that the King had no intention of fulfilling his part of the bargain, though he now possessed the jade.

The Prince resorted to trickery. Addressing the King of Ch'in before his court, he proclaimed that the jade was imperfect; it had a hidden flaw. Enraged, the King demanded that it be pointed out to him. A servant was ordered to bring the jade from the royal treasure house.

With the jade again in his possession, the Prince revealed the King's plot to the audience. Holding the *Pi* high above his head, he yelled, "My humble life may be forfeited, but the *Pi* shall be broken!" The King relented. Under the guise of wrapping the jade, the Prince secretly slipped it to one of his servants, who hastily rode back with it to the King of Chao.

In the second story, set in the middle of the third century B.C., the tyrant Shih Huang Ti ordered Ho's jade carved into a seal. Since it had already been carved into a *Pi*, we must discount one of the two stories. Whether it was Ho's jade or not, the seal was carved and replaced the jade *kuei*, or scepter, as the Imperial symbol. Rubbings, said to be from this seal, read in translation: "With the decree of Heaven, I possess longevity and eternal prosperity." The seal is described as being square, of green and white jade, with a handle of interlocking dragons.

From this time on, wars and bloodshed were the seal's faithful companions. In A.D. 9, when a usurper captured the throne, he knew he could not long reign without the seal, so he plotted to take it from the Dowager Empress. When she refused to surrender it, the plotters used force; in the ensuing struggle the seal was dropped, and one edge was broken.

For nearly two centuries the seal disappeared from sight. It appeared again in A.D. 191, when soldiers found it in the debris of a Han ancestral temple. In the third century A.D. it was possessed by the House of Wei. But not uneventfully, for a treacherous warrior recruited an army and made off with the great stamp. The King of Wei declared war on the thief and sent his armies in pursuit. The warrior escaped by burning the gates of the besieged city where he had been hiding and, running off in the confusion, left the jade behind. He was unsuccessful in his attempt to raise a second army to recapture it.

In A.D. 311 the Ts'in Emperor Huai Ti was captured by barbarians and, before his death sentence was carried out, made to carry the seal through the streets to the new rulers as a symbol of his submission. (In contrast, nearly a thousand years before this a defeated chieftain was made to crawl on his hands and knees through the city, bearing a sacred ring of jade in his mouth, to indicate his submission to the King of Wu. This noble was pardoned, however; poor Huai Ti was not.)

During the bloody years of the Six Dynasties the stone changed hands frequently. Belief in the power of the stone grew stronger as time passed. From its capture by the Northern Chou in A.D. 575 to even after the last Manchu Emperor, in our century, every Chinese ruler possessed the seal; and whether they obtained it by war, intrigue, or inheritance, all seemed to believe this jade to be a divine token of their right to rule.

The great Mongol Khans, Genghis and Kublai, also figured prominently in the seal's eventful history; frequently it passed back and forth between Chinese and Mongol hands. One legendary story tells that in A.D. 1189, when Genghis was proclaimed the Great Khan, for three mornings before the ceremony a lark perched on a square stone in front of Genghis' tent, calling out his name. On the third morning he realized that this was a symbol of divine blessing. Upon this realization the stone split open, revealing the jade seal of state.

This long violent history was not without its moments of beauty. In the eighteenth century, after its having been transmitted from one ruler to another for more than two thousand years, the Emperor Ch'ien Lung threw the seal into the raging waters of the Yangtze River as a sacrifice. The flood ceased, but the seal was lost. Then years later, or so the story goes, one day when the Emperor was sitting beside the waters of the Jade Fountain outside Peking, the seal mysteriously spouted up out of the clear water. The Emperor was so pleased that he dubbed the fountain "The First Spring under Heaven" and had carvers engrave this name upon the rock around the spring.

John Goette, in his *Jade Lore*, calls the jade seal "The Chinese Holy Grail" and notes:

> To understand the symbolism of the jade seal is to have a close insight into the very heart of Chinese administration during 3,000 years. In the sacredness of these insignia of rulership is the kinship of the potentate with Heaven. Just as the Crusaders died by the thousands grasping for the Holy Grail, equal numbers of ancient Chinese have been sacrificed to the retention or capture by force of these precious jades.

On December 5, 1959, many American newspapers carried a short Associated Press item, which read in part: "Communist China announced today it has pardoned Henry Pu-yi, Japan's former puppet Emperor of Manchuria. Since the war he has been imprisoned in Red China on war crimes charges . . ." The article further noted that Henry and the others pardoned at the same time had "repented their crimes and have shown that they are turning over a new leaf." Thus ended another chapter in the story of the last Chinese Emperor to possess the jade seals.

Henry Pu-yi was given the precious jade of Ho in 1908, at the age of two, when under the name Hsüan T'ung he was enthroned as Manchu Emperor of China. The "boy Emperor" was China's last. After being dethroned by the revolutionaries in 1911, he was permitted to retain the seal of state, which, presumably, would have no use or meaning in the new republic.

But when in 1915 Republic President Yüan Shih-k'ai plotted to create a new dynasty and make himself Emperor, he knew that the seal was essential to his plan. Accordingly he planned to steal it, using a relative of the boy Emperor. But his intentions were made public before he could act.

In 1917 a Chinese war lord, General Chang Hsun, attempted to restore the monarchy. Henry, bearing the sacred seal, again ascended the Imperial Dragon Throne but sat there less than two weeks; the general was overthrown. Nine years later the royal treasures were seized, including the jade seal, to become the property of the republic. The Imperial Palace was converted into a museum and the seal was put on display. In 1936, to avoid their seizure by the Japanese, the seal and other treasures were shipped to Shanghai.

Henry, in the meantime, was a not unwilling captive of the

Japanese. In 1934, when they began setting up their puppet state of Manchukuo in Manchuria, they brought Henry out of hiding and with all the impressive ancient Chinese rites proclaimed him Emperor of Manchukuo. All the ritual jades were used, there was no lack of pomp and ceremony, but the jade seal was as bogus as the title—"Emperor Kang Teh."

Henry Pu-yi was captured by the Russians in 1945, then turned over to the Red Chinese.

But what of the fate of the precious jade of Ho, the sacred seal which transmits the state?

No one seems to know, or if they do they aren't talking about it. For, following its shipment to Shanghai, it has never been mentioned among China's treasures. Knowing that this has occurred often in the seal's long eventful history, we shouldn't be too surprised at its seeming disappearance. Nor, considering that it is a stone which for thousands of years established the divine right to rule China, should we wonder why in Communist China today the government is not overly anxious to discuss its existence. Yet, for all we know of life behind the bamboo curtain, it may be that Mao Tse-tung, taking no chances, uses it as a stamp for his official directives.

Plate 15   Animal statues. H: 4⅜". L: 6". Author's collection.

Plate 16   A Ming ceremonial portrait. This solemn gentleman is carrying a jade scepter. He is also wearing a headpiece with jade inserts and from his belt hang various girdle jades. His long fingernails are protected by jade finger sheaths, indicating he is a member of the aristocracy and does not have to labor with his hands. Author's collection.   FACING PAGE

CHAPTER SEVEN

JADEITE: THE MOST SUMPTUOUS JEWEL

The circle divided into the light and the dark, and above and below, a right and left, male and female . . . the world of opposites. These opposites became known under the names yang *and* yin *and created a great stir . . ."*

"The Book of Changes" (*I Ching*)

Owl. A modern carving based on an archaic bronze form. Light green and white jadeite, with brown spots on top of head. H: 12½". W: 7". 20th century. Courtesy M. H. De Young Memorial Museum, San Francisco, California. Avery Brundage collection.

If nephrite was the masculine stone, the essence of Yang, then did there not also exist in nature its opposite, a feminine stone, the essence of Yin, equal in beauty?

I. BURMA'S JADE

1784. Chronologic charts often list a dozen or more major events which occurred in China during the eighteenth century, but this year is never among the dates recorded. To the jade industry, however, 1784 is one of the most important years in its long history, though it took another hundred years or more for most people to realize it.

The year 1784 marked the resumption of trade between China and neighboring Burma, who had been feuding intermittently for nearly twenty years. This would be a relatively unimportant event historically had not one of the items Burma sent China been a large shipment of an unusually hard stone.

This stone, which made its way into the jade carving studios of the Emperor Ch'ien Lung, in many ways resembled nephrite. It was extremely tough, took a high polish, looked almost like nephrite, had to be carved in the same manner, and yet . . . nephrite, when carved and polished, had a bland surface. The new stone was brighter, shinier, and generally more crystalline (in contrast to the oilier, more wax-like appearance of nephrite). Moreover, the new stone occasionally was of a brilliant vivid emerald-green color heretofore unseen in nephrite.

The Burmese called it *kyauksein,* or "green stone." The Chinese named it *fei-ts'ui,* or "kingfisher jade," after the brilliant green plumage of the bird. The name had been used before Sung times, but not after, to denote a certain Khotan nephrite of distinctive green.

It was not until 1863, after extensive chemical tests, that the French scientist Damour announced that the Burmese stone was not nephrite at all and gave it the name by which we know it today: *jadeite.*

The Chinese knew it wasn't the same as soon as they handled it;

it didn't feel the same. And at first they didn't think too highly of it.

In 1800 Chi Yun, a well-known Ch'ing scholar, wrote in his reminiscences that when he was younger "the *fei-ts'ui* jade of Yünnan was not regarded as jade, but as merely usurping the name of jade . . . Now it is regarded as a rare luxury, its price far exceeding that of real jade."

To Chi Yun, despite its price tag, *fei-ts'ui* was still not "real jade." And, surprisingly, not until the beginning of the twentieth century did the Chinese consider and treat it as jade.

The Discovery of Jadeite

When did the Chinese first discover jadeite and begin to use it for carving?

This question of first use is one of the mysteries nephrite and jadeite share in common.

Undoubtedly some jadeite must have come into China before 1784. Chi Yun, for example, implies as much when speaking of when he was younger. Yet there is no record of it, nor have any such dated carvings come to light. Several scholars claim it was mentioned in Chinese annals as early as the T'ang Dynasty, but they appear to be confused over the earlier use of the term *fei-ts'ui*.

Folklore offers its own romantic explanation. S. Howard Hansford, in attempting to find evidence for the story that a Chinese first discovered jadeite in Burma in the thirteenth century, came across the following account, written by a Mr. Warry, a British consular official who visited the jadeite mines in the Kachin Hills in northern Burma in 1888:

> The discovery that green jade of fine quality occurred in Northern Burma was made accidentally by a small Yünnanese trader in the thirteenth century. The story runs that on returning from a journey across the frontier he picked up a piece of stone to balance the load on his mule. The stone proved to be jade of great value and a large party went back to procure more of it. In this errand they were unsuccessful, nobody being able to inform them where the stone occurred. Another attempt, equally fruitless, was made by the Yünnan government in the fourteenth century to discover the stone; all the members of the expedition, it is said, perished by malaria, or at the hands of hostile hill-tribes. From this time onwards, for several cen-

Plate 17 A rare pink jade, one of the few examples known of this color appearing in nephrite. Water cup in the form of a half peach. H: 1½″. L: 3¼″. 18th century. Courtesy Seattle Art Museum, Seattle, Washington. Eugene Fuller collection.

turies, no further exploration in the jade country seems to have been undertaken by the Chinese. Small pieces of the stone occasionally found their way across the frontier, but the exact source of supply continued unknown . . .

Though picturesque (but not beyond belief), Mr. Warry's account must be classified as hearsay until such time as we obtain supporting evidence.

Mining Burmese Jadeite

When jadeite traffic with China was initiated during the reign of the Emperor Ch'ien Lung, most of the stone came from the streams and banks of the Uru River, in the valley at the foot of the Kachin Hills, a dangerously remote area in northern Burma. At first the traffic was confined to water-worn boulders. But it was not long until this supply had been exhausted, and the "Old Mines" in the Kachin Hills were opened.

Jadeite was not found *in place* in this area, however. It had originated high in the hills, over the centuries working its way down with other boulders and rocks to settle in the deep orange clay.

About 1880 jadeite *in place* was discovered on the Tawmaw plateau, sixty-eight miles from Mogaung, Burma. This became the site of the "New Mines," deep quarries which have been the chief source of China's jadeite since that time.

Because of the rainy season, these quarries are workable only three months of the year, from March through May. To keep the mines open for even this brief time, the miners must work from November through February, pumping the veins clear of water. Occasional attempts to keep the mines open longer, by building huge fires at the bottom of the mine shaft and wrapping the miners in wet plantain leaves, have only added to the already shocking fatality rate.

The Second Mystical Gift from Heaven

Though to our knowledge the natives of Burma never carved or used jadeite, there is no lack of native lore concerning it. Burmese tradition claims that far back in prehistory the stone was a mystic gift from Heaven! Special rites are held each spring before the reopening of the mines. Outside of each mine are bamboo houses for the *nats*. The *nats* are spirits of trees, streams, hills, and rocks;

each mine also has its own spirit. All of these must be pampered and placated with offerings before the mining begins each day. New mines are located by means of a divining rod of burning bamboo.

From Burma to China

When jadeite traffic first began, the stone was carried by mule into China through Yünnan Province. (This has led to some confusion, as chroniclers on occasion referred to the stone as *Yünnan jade,* leading some to assume, erroneously, that it was mined in Yünnan Province.) Later, and up to the time of World War II, it was carried by bullock cart to Mogaung and there purchased by jade dealers. Not unlike nephrite, jadeite is subject to special levies and taxes and, up to the time of the Communist Chinese government, was purchased mostly by huge Chinese syndicates. From Mogaung the stone was shipped by river to Rangoon, then by sea to Hong Kong, Canton, and Shanghai.

The World's Greatest Gamble

There is probably no greater gamble than the purchase of jadeite in its uncarved state.

Jadeite is sold in the rough, in boulders varying in weight from one to hundreds of pounds, the outer skin so oxidized that the inside is almost totally hidden. Experienced merchants search the skin to see if it is "pine-flower clad"; i.e., for tiny telltale spots of green. If such are found, they grind away a little of the skin, making a few "open eyes" or "windows" about one inch square. Often the boulder is sold with only this indication of its inner worth. More often than not the buyer finds that the grinder has discovered the boulder's single patch of the precious but fickle emerald green, and the rest of the boulder—due to flaws, fractures, uneven color—may be completely worthless. Sometimes the boulder is sawed in two before it is sold, but again the results may be deceptive; a thin vein of fine jadeite may be revealed on both sides of the split, yet extend no deeper into the stone. The miners are not above practicing deception when they can.

Nor does the deception stop here. Unless the buyer is a member of one of the syndicates, he will attempt in turn to dispose of the stone to a manufacturer or cutter. Only when the stone is finally cut for the carving will its real worth be ascertained.

Plate 18 Jadeite figure of a seated rabbit, wearing a broad belt adorned with skull and crossbones, and a warrior's head in an eagle helmet. To the Aztec the rabbit symbolized excess, and, in this particular carving, drunkenness, a crime which was punished with penalties ranging from degradation to death. It is believed that this figure was carved to commemorate a great victory, when the ban against intoxication was relaxed. Aztec, Mexico. H: 7⅞″. Photograph by Nickolas Muray, courtesy of the Robert Woods Bliss Collection, Washington, D.C. Previously reproduced in *Pre Columbian Art* published by Phaidon Press.

It is said that only one stone in ten thousand is really good, yet before World War II over six thousand were bought each year, many for phenomenally high prices.

John Wenti Chang, from his long experience in the arts of buying and cutting jade, has put it succinctly: "In this market, success comes only to those blessed with sound technical judgment, nimble wit, and shrewd cunning, and even then only when the Goddess of Fortune does not turn away."

The Colors of Jadeite

More than any other quality, it is the color of jadeite that distinguishes it from nephrite and makes it unusually precious

The brilliant Imperial or emerald green (jadeite's most highly prized hue) is only one of its many colors, and certainly not its most common. Jadeite ranges from pure white through a spectrum of grays, yellows, red-browns, into an inconceivable number of shades of green, through blue to black. Mellow blue and mauve jadeite are especially appreciated by the Chinese. Often several colors will appear in a single piece, enabling the carver, for example, to create leaves, stems, and flowers in varying tones. The lavender-green combination seems to be peculiar to jadeite, as do several blues, purples, and reds.

Like nephrite, pure jadeite would be colorless—color comes from the presence of other minerals in the stone. Yet when comparing the colors of nephrite and jadeite it becomes doubly evident that we are dealing with two separate stones. Conceivably, were we to possess a piece of nephrite and a piece of jadeite with an identical amount of chemical colorization, the two would appear to be of different shades. For the brightness and clarity of jadeite's tones contrast sharply with the soapy, almost aged-looking hues of most pieces of nephrite. Jadeite comes closer to being, and sometimes is, translucent. In general, one might say that the colors of jadeite tend toward vividness and translucency, while the hues of nephrite are greasier, denser, and heavier. Nephrite looks soft, jadeite hard.

Jadeite's finest color is Imperial or emerald green. Often a ring with a perfect cabochon of this shade will sell for from ten to fifteen thousand dollars. In appearance, such a stone does resemble a fine emerald (both owe their color to the presence of chromium), but why compliment the emerald when a perfect piece of jade of this hue is infinitely rarer? Actually, the best comparison is to the St. Patrick's Day ties of Kelly green.

A Debunking: The Uses and Dating of Jadeite

Though jadeite might be termed a modern stone in so far as the Chinese are concerned, having been imported into China in quantity only since 1784, we know less about it, in some respects, than the older nephrite.

Because portions of this section contradict opinions held by some jade experts and merchants, it might be best to note first the manner in which these facts were gathered and confirmed.

All available accounts regarding jadeite were checked and double-checked. This resulted in the collection of a number of contradictory and highly debatable opinions, especially with regard to dating.

Antique Jadeite?

For example, jade catalogues published by some contemporary dealers attribute to jadeite the one thing it does not possess; antiquity. It also seems to be common practice to assign to the Ch'ien Lung period every beautiful object carved in jadeite, whatever its form, even though it was only during the last ten years of Ch'ien Lung's reign that any appreciable quantity of the stone was brought into China.

This is, of course, a less serious error than the uncommonly explicit designations of one dealer-author, who lists one jadeite vase as early Ch'ien Lung period, circa A.D. 1745; a pair of white jadeite bowls as circa 1700; another vase and a censer as K'ang Hsi period (1662–1722); and a cicada carving as Sung Dynasty (960–1279)—and who speaks of archaic rituals objects of *jadeite*.

Perhaps ignorance is an excuse; certainly a veneer of antiquity makes the merchandise seem more valuable, provided the purchaser is sufficiently gullible.

In an attempt to debunk some of these modern myths of jadeite, pertinent questions regarding the stone were submitted to the foremost jade dealers of Hong Kong, men who have spent their lives working with jade and whose families, often for many generations, have been active in the art. Every Monday evening these dealers meet privately in Hong Kong to discuss the jade business. These are their conclusions regarding the "antiquity" and uses of jadeite, as expressed by Y. K. Ma of Kowloon, descendant of a long line of jade dealers and himself the head of a large jade firm.

The Age of Jadeite

1. Burmese jadeite was not introduced into China in quantity prior to the 1780s. Small amounts may have come in earlier, but there was no extensive amount of carving.

The Uses of Jadeite

2. Burmese jadeite, and particularly the fine green of jewel quality, was first used chiefly for jewelry: thumb rings, hat tubes, buttons, buckles, collar ornaments, etc. While there undoubtedly were some important exceptions, it was not until after the jade quarry was established, about 1880, that the craftsmen started using the jadeite for large ornamental pieces. (As discussed in Chapter Eight, the introduction of a faster cutting abrasive played an important part in this transition.) *Generally, the beautiful green jadeite censers, bowls, and vases were neither produced nor on the market until about the turn of this century (1900).*

These Chinese jade experts agree that during the last years of the reign of the Emperor Ch'ien Lung and for many years thereafter *fine* jadeite was used *almost exclusively* for jewelry. Fine jadeite has always been rare, even rarer than the finest nephrite. The much-coveted spots of Imperial green are infrequent. When a piece of this exceptional material was found, it was carved, therefore, not into a large object, but into thumb rings, bracelets, hat tubes, and other small objects, which not only commanded a much higher price but were far more appropriate to the limited size of the jewel spots. The clippings or sawed-off sections in which there was little or no green were sometimes used for desk ornaments. These, chiefly in white jadeite, could date back to the last part of the eighteenth century. It was not until about 1900, when the new supplies of the quarried apple-green jadeite increased the material available, that the craftsmen could use it for larger ornaments and larger carvings. (Unquestionably there were a few exceptions.)

Mr. Ma tells how a dealer was once approached by a Palace eunuch who had stolen a carved jadeite plate from the palace. It was late Ch'ien Lung or early nineteenth century. The plate had a superb center section of emerald-green jadeite of the finest quality; the rest of the material was of inconsequential value. The dealer "accidentally" dropped the plate, breaking it; he then offered to buy it for a fraction of its previous price. Since the thief couldn't report him and believed the broken plate to be worthless, he consented to the sale. The wily dealer then cut out the undamaged central "jewel spot," recut it into jewelry, and resold it for a fabulous profit.

Religious Uses of Jadeite?

3. Burmese jadeite was *never* used for religious, ritual, or burial purposes. Only the traditional nephrite was so used. To the Chinese, nephrite was the stone of Heaven; jadeite was the stone of Burma. They not only knew the difference, they strictly observed it.

The Graduated Bead Necklaces

4. It will perhaps come as a surprise to some merchants and collectors that the beautiful graduated jade necklaces to which they attribute antiquity probably came into being no earlier than the turn of this century, and as a result of European influence.

The 108 beads of the well-known Mandarin chain were of uniform size, generally 11 to 12 millimeters in diameter. Goette estimates that at the height of the Ch'ing Dynasty approximately half a million mandarins were entitled to wear these beads. The Boxer Rebellion (1900) and the subsequent influx of Westerners had a tremendous impact on the jade industry. Not only did the long-nosed Western barbarians of the Victorian era crave large imposing jade carvings, they were also eager for Imperial green stones and necklaces. They did not require uniform strands. The result was the copying of European pearl-style necklaces in jadeite. John Wenti Chang joins the Hong Kong dealers in agreeing that the graduated necklaces of jade did not exist earlier than 1900. They were made primarily for the Westerners. Of course it was much simpler to find 101 matching beads of varying sizes than to find 108 large uniform ones.

And what effect has this debunking of jadeite's "antiquity" on the stone itself? It leaves its vivid colors, its superb carving, its marvelous pieces not one whit diminished in their brilliance. For, like nephrite, jadeite must be evaluated on the inherent quality of the stone and the consummate artistry of its carvers. Using the most rigid standards of excellence, it is evident that many jadeite pieces, carved in our own times, compare favorably with the finest antique pieces carved in the traditional nephrite. Age itself has no value. Do we treasure old diamonds more than new? It is the same with jade.

Equally important, the honest dating of jadeite should dispel the myth that jade carving entered into a permanent decline when Ch'ien Lung's reign ended. In reality, it took on an added dimension. The Chinese artists applied their traditional techniques and skills to the new stone with its fresh color combinations. They faced new challenges, found new uses, rejected others. The fortuitous color clouds and spots of jadeite made possible multi-colored cameo-like carvings, superb jewelry, and actually inaugurated a new period of jade design and craftsmanship. It may well be that the modern era will prove to be one of the most impressive in the long history of the art.

Mask. Formerly owned by President Porfirio Díaz. Light green and white jadeite. H: 2¾". Classic Teotihuacan, Mexico. Courtesy National Gallery of Art, Washington, D.C. Robert Woods Bliss collection.

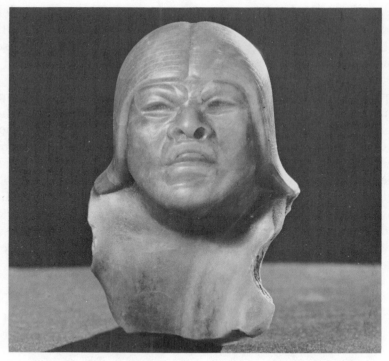

Bust of a man. One of the finest pre-Columbian jade carvings known. Note the simplicity and strength of the modeling. Blue jadeite. H: 2¾". Olmec, Mexico. Courtesy National Gallery of Art, Washington, D.C. Robert Woods Bliss collection.

II. PRE-COLUMBIAN JADE

Two great civilizations grew up around jade, giving it a prominent place in their worship, holding it high in their esteem, uncovering its beauty, attributing to it supernatural qualities, endowing it with more myths, legends, and power than have ever been accorded any other stone.

The stone of the Chinese was nephrite; that of the pre-Columbians, jadeite. Independent of each other, these two cultures discovered and carved the two faces of jade. That there are striking similarities in their beliefs regarding the stone is one of the great mysteries.

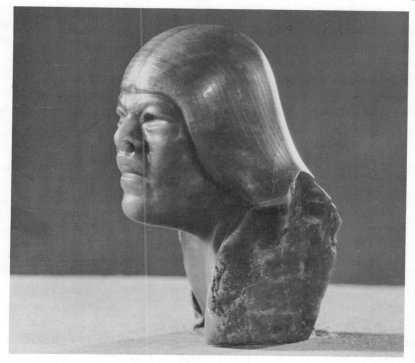

Side view of illustration on opposite page.

Jadeite and the Pre-Columbians

Jadeite may have been new to China in the eighteenth century, but in the civilizations of Mexico, Central and South America it had been carved and appreciated long before the voyage of Columbus in 1492.

It had many ornamental, utilitarian, and religious uses. Jade knives drew the blood of human sacrifices. Jade masks turned ordinary men into vengeful gods. Myth says that the mother of the Aztec god Quetzalcoatl was made pregnant when she swallowed a piece of jade. Body jades accompanied the dead to the grave to prevent decomposition! Jade was consumed in powdered form to assure immortality! Worn next to the skin, it cured disease and warded off evil entities!

In the pre-Columbian art remains, we have perhaps an even fuller history of the beginning of the jade carver's art than has to date come from China. Jade weapons, probably the first objects carved of jadeite, including axes, celts, spears, and knives, were in use up to the time of the Spanish conquest in the early sixteenth century.

This was a highly advanced civilization. Bernal Díaz del Castillo, the soldier-chronicler of Cortés, wrote in *The Discovery and Conquest of Mexico* of first sighting the Vale of Anahuac and Lake Texcoco, where the Aztec capital stood:

> When we saw so many cities and villages built in the waters of the lake and other large towns on dry land, and that straight, level causeway leading into Mexico City, we were amazed and we said that it was like the enchanted things related in the book of Amadis, because of the huge towers, temples, and buildings rising from the water, and all of masonry. And some of the soldiers even asked whether the things we saw were not a dream.

Today we can feel the same wonder and awe when we view the marvelous jades of this civilization, which include flasks, bowls, cups; masks, earplugs, rings, necklaces, all manner of jewelry; skulls and skullcaps; heads and full figures in the round, ceremonial carvings; pendants, plaques, and numerous objects with jade inlay. They even bettered the Chinese by one use: tubular jade beads worn by the women to support their breasts.

But the jade carver's art in the Americas never reached the high stage of development it reached in Asia. There are no large vases, no intricately detailed carvings, no plates of paper thinness. The Spaniards came, and, for all the pros and cons of both sides, the art died.

Montezuma, Cortés, and Jade

"I will give you some very valuable stones, which you will send to your ruler in my name," Montezuma, the Aztec Emperor, told Cortés. "They are Chalchithils and are not to be given to anyone but to him, your great prince. Each stone is worth two loads of gold."

But the Chalchithils, or jades, as well as most of Cortés' treasure never reached their destination. Two of the three treasure ships were captured by the French pirate Jean Florin; none of the jade is on record as having reached Spain.

Another story, to which several authors have ascribed authenticity, again unites this trio. It is said that though Montezuma was virtually a prisoner of Cortés he was treated as an honored guest. Each day the two were accustomed to play a native game which resembled chess, at the conclusion of which they would exchange gifts.

One day, at the close of the game, Montezuma presented his jailer with several large disks of gold and silver; then, noting Cortés' great pleasure, announced: "Tomorrow I shall give you a gift which will make these disks seem as no more than a single tile in the roadway."

Needless to say, to Cortés the night seemed long, the day longer, and the game itself longer still. When the game was finally ended the Aztec Emperor summoned his royal treasurer, who came bearing a large silver tray.

On it were three beads of perfect jade.

Cortés reacted with "bitter disappointment."

Montezuma then explained that jades were his most precious possession, that in order of importance he valued jade, turquoise, the long green plumes of the quetzal bird, and then, finally, gold.

Perhaps this eased the conscience of the gold-plundering Cortés, who appears to have been far less impressed with jade than Bernal Díaz. Díaz, with more foresight, took jade as well as gold in his sacking. Once, when captured by Indians, it was the jade that ransomed his life.

Antiquity and Carving

In Central Mexico, in what we call the proto-classic or formative archaic culture, existing before 1500 B.C., the carving of jade was already an accomplished art. Up to the time of the Spanish conquest jade seems to have been cut by primitive methods—string sawing, with sharp sand, emery, or pumice as the abrasive; the holes drilled with cactus. No metal was used! Yet no one could call the products of this art crude after viewing the fantastic jades in the Robert Woods Bliss collection now in the National Gallery in Washington, D.C., many of which appear in the handsome Phaidon Press book, *Pre-Columbian Art*.

Similarities in the Pre-Columbian and Chinese Uses of Jade

Miguel Covarrubias, in his excellent *Indian Art of Mexico and Central America*, notes that "the Classic Maya had a passion for fine emerald-green jade, delicately carved and highly polished.

Highly polished figure of a man. Green jadeite. H: 9⅛". Olmec, Mexico.
Courtesy National Gallery of Art, Washington, D.C. Robert Woods Bliss
collection.

The Maya chiefs in reliefs and paintings are always shown wearing all sorts of jade ornaments . . ."

Covarrubias' description of the discovery of the royal burial chamber of Palenque might, with few changes, describe the opening of a Chinese tomb. The Mayans appear to have been even more lavish than the Chinese in their use of jade for burial purposes:

> The personage for whom the tomb was constructed, whose crumbling bones were found in an enormous, massive sarcophagus hollowed out of a single block of stone, was covered with objects of jade which gleamed in brilliant green on the layer of red cinnabar with which the corpse had been painted. On his head he wore a band garnished with large jade spangles; the locks of his hair were held in place by jade tubes; his face was covered by a magnificent mask of jade mosaic with eyes of shell and obsidian; and on his ears he wore a pair of jade earplugs incised with glyphs. His shoulders were covered with a great collar of rows of tubular jade beads, and around his neck there was a precious necklace of beads in the form of calabashes alternating with jade blossoms. His wrists were bound with long strings of jade beads forming cuffs, and on each finger he wore a jade ring, nine of them plain, one carved with the most exquisite delicacy in the shape of a little crouching man. He held a great jade ball in one hand, a square dice of jade in the other. There was a fine jade buckle or loincloth ornament, and by his feet was a jade statuette of the sun god.

The Land Bridge

Was there at one time, as some contend, a land bridge between the American continent and China over which the Chinese traveled, bringing with them both jade and the art of its carving?

Striking similarities in several arts and crafts of the two civilizations have helped to keep this question alive.

Those who have advanced this theory might find their bridge a little shaky if they build it, as some have attempted to do, exclusively on jade. For nearly all of the pre-Columbian jade is jadeite, which was unknown to the early Chinese, so far as we know. The jadeite of Mexico and the Americas also differs chemically from the jadeite of Burma, in that it possesses traces of diopside, a complex silicate, *which does not appear in Burmese jadeite.* Though it seems inconceivable, experts claim that the Meso-American jadeite, now believed to have been obtained from Yucatan, also has a greater range of colors and texture than the Burmese jadeite.

It is of interest that the emerald-green jadeite known in China as *fei-ts'ui*, after the colored feathers of the kingfisher, is also the most prized color in Meso-American jades, known to the Aztecs as *quetzalitztli*, after the vivid green plumage of the quetzal.

The Mysteries

Why did these two great civilizations both hold the jade stone in such reverence?

Our only safe conclusion, from present evidence, is that the pre-Columbians, as well as the Chinese, found a precious stone of singular quality and learned to work it into objects of uncommon beauty; that they also sought not the most common material but one of the rarest, whose refractory nature drew forth their greatest skill as craftsmen.

That both the Chinese and the pre-Columbians believed jade would exorcise demons, heal the sick, prevent decomposition, and, when swallowed, confer immortality are paradoxes whose solution lies carefully hidden within the two stones known as jade.

CHAPTER EIGHT

THE ANONYMOUS ARTISTS

Statue of a female animal in full-round. Brown and white nephrite. H: 4″.
Sung Dynasty. Courtesy M. H. De Young Memorial Museum, San
Francisco, California. Avery Brundage collection.

If jade is not polished it cannot be made worth anything. If man does not suffer trials he cannot be purified.

Chinese proverb

It is time we turned to those men whose magic transformed the world's toughest stone into beautiful objects of art, and to the techniques by which this magic was effected.

Early Jade Carving

How was jade first carved?

As with almost every aspect of Chinese life, there is an explanation in the folklore of the Celestial Kingdom. John Wenti Chang tells the story in his own words:

> While searching the river bed, a workman once found a strange new stone, hard, heavy, close-grained. It seemed fit to work. But days of diligent effort failed to dislodge the tiniest flake. Only the tools broke, the hardest chisels from the toughest flint.
>
> In distress the workman consulted his Chieftain, a man well known for his wisdom and intelligence. This one considered the new stone and the broken tools. At last he spoke thus: "It is apparent that this material is harder than any other that the God of the Earth has given us, therefore we have nothing hard enough to chip it. However, see you how the God of the River has worked it for his use. With water and sand he has worn it round. Do you therefore take water and sand and work it likewise."

In such manner, it is said, was born the use of abrasives, the most important step in man's mastery of the stone. By merely adding the simple tools of the jade craftsmen—the saws, drills, and disks—we have the fundamentals of the craft.

Jade's Technical Evolution

It is doubtful whether the technical evolution of any other art or craft was so simple. You can count on the fingers of one hand the major technical changes which have occurred between the beginning of jade carving, more than three thousand years ago, and today. First, a change in abrasives, from sand to crushed garnets. Next, the introduction of metal tools, occurring, we believe, during the Chou Dynasty, about 500 B.C. (Hansford: "As regards essential tools and tactics, the craft had reached its maturity by the end of the Chou Dynasty.") Third, another switch in abrasives, this time from garnets to corundum, in about the twelfth century A.D. Fourth, sometime after 1891, the change from corundum to carborundum. And, last, the introduction of electricity and power-driven tools, occurring in the twentieth century.

Water, Sand, and a Piece of String

Though we don't know how jade was first cut, we can hazard a good guess. Ironically, jade, the world's toughest stone, can be cut with water, sand, and a piece of string. The sand and water are spread on the stone as abrasives, the string is then drawn back and forth across the surface like a saw. Holes can be drilled through jade by using sand, water, and the rotating action of a piece of *bamboo.*

Admittedly, this is not a fast method of cutting, but neither is the use of a metal wire and abrasives, the method used from about 500 B.C. to the present day. Patience would appear to be a major attribute in jade carving, for often a craftsman will spend years on a single carving. Possibly it was a carver addicted to wishful thinking who gave birth to one of the most persistent of the carving myths, that of the Chinese Excalibur.

The Sword That Cuts Jade

From about the third century B.C. there are frequent references in Chinese texts to the *K'un-wu* sword or knife. According to *The Records of Chou*, the sovereign Mu Wang, on one of his expeditions, was presented "cloth that could withstand fire and a sword that could cut jade. When this cloth was soiled it needed only to be cleaned in fire, while jade cut by that sword became soft as wool." Other texts say that this sword would "cut jade like clay" or make it possible for it to be "worked like wax." But then the story changes slightly. A fifteenth-century account reads: "There are ancient jades, rare and especially finely worked, that cannot, it seems, have been carved by humans and are generally reported to be the work of spirits . . . But I myself think not: they are all cut by means of the *K'un-wu* knife and toad-grease . . ." Hansford, in tracing this and similar references, found that "toad-grease" was an oily substance that works better than water in holding the abrasive to the surface of the stone. It may also, at one time, have contained an abrasive substance.

But the *K'un-wu,* the sword that cuts jade, was it altogether a product of the imagination and nothing more?

The answer may lie in a glass case in the Anthropological Museum in Victoria, British Columbia. Here rests what may be an original *K'un-wu* sword (except called by a different name, as it was used in prehistoric times by the natives of British Columbia). Discovered in a cave in the Fraser River area were two objects: a boulder of nephrite with V-shaped marks cut across the top, and a sheet of sandstone, the end of which fits the grooves in the boulder. By applying water and sawing with the sandstone, which supplied its own abrasive sand, the natives of this area (and those of China as well) may have cut jade before the advent of more effective tools.

In summary, *the secret of cutting jade lies not so much in the tools used as the abrasive.* And from the earliest stage of the development of this art known to us, the Chinese were paying special attention to this substance.

Abrasives

As shown above, sandstone and quartz sand, readily available in most parts of China, were probably the first abrasives. Crushed garnets came into use sometime later but did not entirely replace quartz sand, which is still used today in some phases of jade carving.

The discovery of corundum for this use seems to have occurred during the twelfth century A.D., about the time Kublai Khan first arrived in China. Corundum (emery or "black sand") requires careful preparation; the right grade of sand must be obtained and crushed to the desired consistency. Some have surmised that the great Khan brought corundum with him or taught the Chinese how to make it.

There is another, more likely explanation. With the Tartar conquest, a new source of abrasive sand was opened up in the Ta-t'ung region, along the Mongolian borderland. One hundred and six families were sent there annually to obtain this sand, used for grinding jade. Since there were many sources of quartz sand closer to Peking, we must assume that there was something special about the Ta-t'ung sand. Did these families manufacture corundum, the hardest of natural abrasives except the diamond?

If so, it would account for the carving during the Yüan period of huge objects such as the wine bowls described by Friar Oderic.

However, there is no mention of this substance in the records of the Ming period, only during Ching times, when it was in general use in all of the jade shops of Peking. Might the rebuilding of the Great Wall of China, which put this particular area outside the borders of China proper, account for the temporary loss of this effective abrasive?

Carborundum (technically, crystallized carbide of silicon) was first artificially prepared in 1891 in the United States. The date of its importation into China remains elusive; however, it is evident that the Chinese took immediate notice of it, for it is often called "Canton sand," named for the port where the first shipment landed. Its use did much to speed modern jade carving and certainly had its influence on the cutting of larger, more involved decorative pieces. There are some who feel carborundum was a dubious blessing. The slower abrasives gave a greater control; when the tool or drill slipped, there was little chance of damage, for cutting occurred only after long application. The faster carborundum meant less control. On examining many of the older jades one finds that even the most minute lines are sure, with no accidental crossing, no rough edges on the carving. Under the slower abrasives, the peculiar texture of nephrite, its fibrous hard-soft-hard-soft composition gave way evenly. On some (but by no means all) of the newer jades the opposite is true. Carborundum often gouges out tiny ridges, discernible when feeling the surface or under close visual inspection.

Pao Yao: The Mysterious Powder

Pao yao, the "precious powder" used for the final polish, was for many years the most closely guarded secret of the jade carver's art. It is a fine gray powder, gritty to the feel. Some claimed it was made from crushed rubies or sapphires; they called it "jewel dust."

Hansford dispelled this pleasing illusion by having samples analyzed and finding that it consisted of fine carborundum, diluted with "what appears to be calcareous silt, or with loess." Yet *pao yao* was used long before carborundum came into China. Perhaps its ingredients have changed (from corundum to carborundum). This would also account for the high gloss on many of the twentieth-century jades.

FROM MOUNTAIN TO CARVING

To see how jade is carved, let's follow the stone from when it was first discovered in Chinese Turkestan.

High in the mountains of Khotan, a large block of nephrite is cracked from the earth, transported by mules down to the lower valleys, shipped by freighter to the port of Canton.

It is a crude, uneven block of stone. Roughly cut, it gives to only the experienced the clues to its hidden nature. Yet many men have already handled it and quietly assessed its value. Veins of color (but how deep?), evidence of a fracture (one or many?), a slice of marvelous texture (an exception or the rule?); point by point the virtues and faults of the particular stone are mentally tabulated, then converted into currency.

If a Chinese jade syndicate has already purchased it at the mines it will go straight to its destination, one of the jade shops. If not, it will be placed on the open market for auction.

Bidding for Jade

There is nothing quite like a Chinese jade auction, unless it is a football game.

On the day before the auction, the blocks of uncut jade are numbered and put on display in the importing house. During the day each stone will be examined by hundreds of merchants, and each face will be a mask of disinterest.

On the day of the auction the distinguished auctioneer (*sin sang*) stands amid the merchants, dressed in a large coat with extra-long sleeves. Generally he is a very large man, for good reason.

The merchants are quiet, expressionless.

The auctioneer plants his feet solidly on the ground, takes a deep breath, and announces the number of the first stone.

Suddenly the merchants surge forward, all frantically trying to reach into the long sleeves and grasp the auctioneer's hand, to convey their bids in finger talk. It is all in pantomime; not a word is spoken. Not only must the auctioneer manage to keep his balance, but he must also remember every bid and who made it, then decide when a satisfactory offer has been received. Shouting the name of the fortunate bidder, he straightens his robe, adjusts his stance, takes another deep breath, and announces the number of the next stone.

No price is ever mentioned aloud. No man ever knows what his neighbor bid. Only the auctioneer knows the details of each transaction, and this is not recorded on paper but in his head.

To qualify as a *sin sang* a man must possess three qualities: great strength, a tremendous memory, and a deep knowledge of the worth of rough jade.

What Does It Contain?

The boulder is then transported to the yard of the shop which bought it. Here it is again examined carefully, this time by the owner of the shop and his chief artisan. They measure and consider the block, asking the same questions as the men who first purchased it, but adding considerations of what it might contain. Two vases? Possibly. Or maybe several small bowls. The flaw indicates that it could not be carved into a single large piece. Besides, at the present time there is no market for a carving of that size.

On occasion pieces have been studied for more than a year before being cut. No two pieces are exactly alike, though they may have adjoined each other in the earth.

The piece is finally, carefully marked for sawing.

Sawing

Three men work in sawing the stone. Two work the saw (*la ssŭ-tzŭ*), which consists of a single strand of wire, generally notched, and drawn taut in a bamboo frame. With a ladle a third man supplies the wet abrasive mixture which does the actual cutting. After biting into the jade, the abrasive flows down into a bowl set to receive it, since it will be used again and again, until it contains too much jade dust to grip effectively.

Weeks, even months, of constant, persistent, backbreaking sawing may be necessary before the stone is cut into the desired pieces.

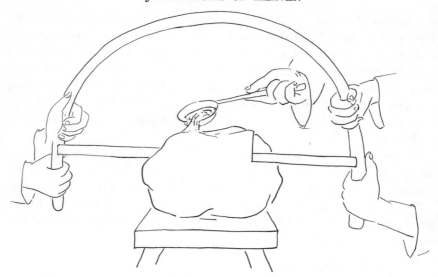

*After the boulder has been carefully examined, it is cut in the yard of the shop.
Two men work the saw (la ssŭ-tzŭ) while a third supplies the wet abrasive
mixture that does the actual cutting.*

Inking the Design

The artisan now takes one of the pieces and studies it. Only
after much thought and insight does he ink the design on the stone
and pass it on to the rougher.

Years of training as an apprentice and years of experience as a
carver are necessary before a man is permitted to see in the stone
its hidden design, before he becomes a jade artist. Pan Ping-Heng,
a modern jade carver, has described one phase of this training:
"When I was an apprentice, my master trained me to imagine that
the clouds were stones and to design objects from them according
to their shape and color. Carvers are also trained to see these
things in the grain of wood or in the pattern of shadows."

Roughing It

The rougher now cuts the stone along the desired lines. To do so,
he uses both his feet and hands. His feet operate the treadle which
spins the cutting wheel; his left hand holds and moves the stone
under the wheel, while his right feeds abrasive onto the surface to
be cut. If it is a large piece, another man will feed the abrasive.
An exceptionally large boulder will be suspended from the ceiling of

the shop on wires. The wheels, which vary considerably in size, are generally of steel or iron. But again it is the abrasive which does most of the work, the actual cutting. The artisan frequently re-examines the stone—watching for flaws, any sudden changes in color or consistency, as he re-marks it.

When a pebble (rather than a boulder or block) is used for carving, the initial process differs slightly, in that the oxidized "skin" is ground off before the design is applied, except when the skin is used as part of the design.

Drilling, Gouging, and Grinding

Once roughed and again marked, the stone is then passed to a man operating a larger grinding wheel (*mo t'o*), who grinds down

Once the boulder is cut into smaller pieces, these pieces are again studied, then further defined on the cutting wheel. Again it is the abrasive that does most of the work.

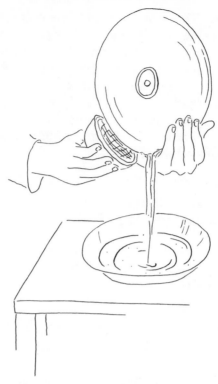

One man operates the large grinding wheel (mo t'o) which grinds the rough jade down to the desired shape, in this case a small bowl.

the rough edges, feeding the abrasive with his left hand, holding the stone against the wheel with his right. Smaller grinding wheels (*ya t'o*) further define the object's shape.

Jade is never actually *carved;* it is *ground,* until only the desired form or shape remains. The statement of one of the carvers, quoted earlier, bears repetition here: "Our job is to subtract; we cannot add."

Past this point the tools of the individual jade craftsmen vary considerably, depending upon their specialty and their ingenuity in designing and making tools. Undercutting and relief work are done with mounted vertical drills (*chuang ting*). For hollowing vases and bowls, a tubular drill (*la tsuan*) is used. The jade is held firmly, and the tubular drill (filled with abrasive sand and water) is rotated into the stone with the use of a small bow. When the desired depth is reached, the hollow drill is removed, the core broken off with a sharp blow of a hammer and chisel. The toughness of jade makes this an exacting process; the carver must know exactly where to hit, from what angle, and how hard.

Another method for hollowing a bowl consists of making deep parallel lineal cuts into the center of the stone with a cutting disk, then breaking off the material between the cuts, and finally grinding down what remains to achieve an even interior.

Detail work and surface decoration are usually done with drills or small cutting disks (*kou t'o*). The diamond is used only in the diamond-point drill—for the cutting of poetic inscriptions, common during Ch'ien Lung's time but in less demand today—and in the power-driven diamond saw, a relatively recent innovation, used mostly for the preliminary cutting of the stone.

Step by step, the craftsmen and the artist, working in close collaboration, bring the stone to its finished form, in this case as a superbly wrought bowl of the beautiful green and white com-

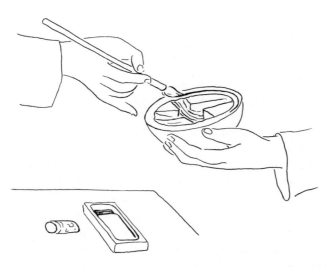

At each stage the artist studies the piece and re-inks the design. Here he is outlining what will be the lip of the bowl. This bowl is being hollowed by making deep parallel cuts in the center with a cutting disk, then breaking off the material between the cuts. The remainder will then be ground down to achieve an even interior.

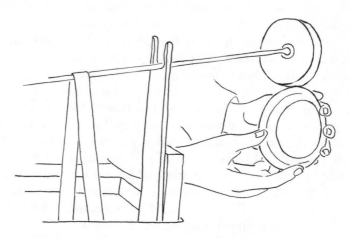

A small cutting disk (kou t'o) *is used for the detail work and surface decoration. The craftsman in this drawing is working on the rim of the bowl.*

bination that the Chinese describe as "moss-entangled-in-snow."

Yet even now, after months of labor by many specialists, perhaps thousands of man-hours, the object is not finished. There remains one final exacting process, during which the finest carving may be rendered mediocre or a work of art. This is the polishing.

Polishing

The first stage in polishing is the rubbing down of the jade to make the surface uniformly even. This is done with the *chiao t'o,* a curious tool that at first glance looks like the large grinding wheel but is really a molded form composed of the finest-grade carborundum and shellac. This is rotated on the lathe, the jade held against it, the tool supplying its own abrasive.

Next the entire surface of the jade is smeared with a paste made of the previously mentioned *pao yao* and water. Leather buffing wheels of various sizes polish most of the carving. To reach the most remote surfaces, tiny leather plugs are used.

Every scratch, every sharp angle must be removed and the world's toughest stone made to look as soft as molded clouds, as flawless as if a creation of the imagination, its surface so pure that it seems one is looking right into the heart of the stone.

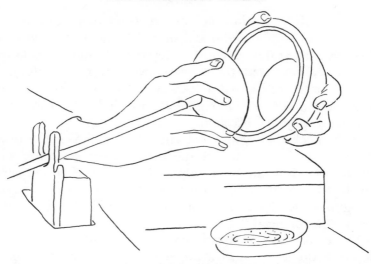

The first stage in polishing the finished jade is rubbing down the piece with the chiao t'o. This tool, which resembles a grinding wheel, is actually a molded form composed of the finest-grade carborundum and shellac, thereby supplying its own abrasive.

THE ANONYMOUS ARTISTS

Who were the great artists of jade—the Chinese Donatellos, Michelangelos, and Rodins? Who conceived the marvelous horse's head of green jade which today rests in London's Victoria and Albert Museum, or the fateful jade seals of state, or the first *Pi*, or the first *Ts'ung*, or the detailed screens of the era of Ch'ien Lung?

We don't know. No personalities, no names, no hallmarks disclose the identity of the jade artists.

Their anonymity is our loss. If carvings were signed we might discover that a single artist was responsible for a wholly new style of carving, that apprentices to this artist further developed his ideas until they became the styles of the period, that certain works were representative of their times and others far ahead of them. Not only could we distinguish between the innovators and the imitators, but gone would be many of the anachronistic mysteries of jade. And how much easier it would be to date it!

We know the general pattern of the jade carver's life: that he was early apprenticed, probably by the age of fourteen; that he spent many years learning his trade, finally becoming a craftsman,

sometimes with good fortune an artist-designer, and in exceptional cases owner of a studio and shop. We know too that he often
reached his peak at thirty, began to deteriorate, sometimes losing his
sight at forty, and that there were few carvers over fifty. With
reason, for until well into this century there were six days in his
working week and twelve to eighteen hours in his working day, and
his was hard, physical exertion.

There is much that we do not know about him or the development of his craft. When did the artist-carver separate, so that
two men instead of one were responsible for the finished carving?
When did this number increase to several? When did specializa-
tion begin, so a given artist or carver would do only vases or
flower designs or beads?

We have already discussed some of the anthropological, religious, aesthetic, and historical aspects of jade; but this separation
is deceptive, for all these lines, currents, and forces merged into
one focal point, the jade artist. It is in his hands, his brain, his
heart that the conception of the finished carving took place.
Trained in his art, with inherent reverence toward the stone,
familiar with its traditional forms, it was he who often turned the
world's toughest stone into a carving of consummate artistry.

Many aspects of his craft were traditional. Yet no two pieces of
jade were the same; each was in itself a new challenge. His greatest
talent lay in his acute sensitivity to the stone.

His design had to reveal the picture already created but
hidden by nature. He had to know the stone intimately, aware
of every flaw and imperfection, intuitively sensing its concealed
virtues and potentialities. He was constantly aware of its limitations,
yet knew he could do with this material what could never be done
with any other. During the many months between his first exam-
ination of the roughhewn stone and its last polishing he had to be
aware of its every changing mood. He had to know it, the Chinese
say, "as a husband should know his wife."

His eyes had to be able to see below the surface of the stone,
judging how far a streak of color would penetrate, in which
direction it would turn.

His ear had to be able to distinguish from the different sounds
of grinding exactly what was taking place within the stone.

His fingers had to see for him when his eyes could not, since
often the abrasive hid the surface of the stone.

Thousands of years ago the Indian sage Vijnanabhiksu wrote that "the statue, already existing in the block of stone, is only revealed by the sculptor."

Yet how few could truly reveal it, and how great is our debt that they could!

The Chinese Romeo and Juliet

The jade artist is anonymous to us today, but in his own time he was often known to his contemporaries by his distinctive style. And so comes to us one of the few legends connected with the jade artist, a story as well known to the Chinese as is the story of Romeo and Juliet to us.

Once upon a time there was a poor young jade carver, in love with a rich man's daughter. The girl's father forbade the courtship, but, young and in love, the pair eloped anyway.

To do this the young man had to give up his art, since his style was so unique that any object he carved would reveal his identity.

But one day his beloved fell sick. Without money to purchase medicine, his only alternative was his art. He carved a beautiful goddess in green jade, then sold it, on condition that the merchant who purchased it never reveal how he obtained it.

As fate would have it, the girl's father was an avid collector of jade, and the piece soon fell into his hands. Instantly recognizing the style, he offered the merchant a huge bounty to reveal the whereabouts of the carver. And although no merchant would commit such a deed except in fiction, this merchant weakened.

The father found the pair, killed the young man, and took his daughter home.

But late one night the girl took the jade goddess and fled again to the site of her great happiness. Digging up the grave, she threw herself into the arms of her beloved, there to wait until death came upon her.

But when the moon rose a curious thing happened. The spirit of the young man, which had taken refuge in the cool jade goddess, moved back into the inert body and the lover lived again.

At this moment the father arrived. So overcome was he by the miracle that he welcomed the young man as his son and accepted the couple into his home and heart. The jade goddess was given as an offering to a nearby temple, where it is said to reside today, its very presence a comfort to all young lovers.

CHAPTER NINE

MODERN JADE

The Superior Man competes in virtue with jade.

"The Book of Rites" (*Li Chi*)
Chou Dynasty

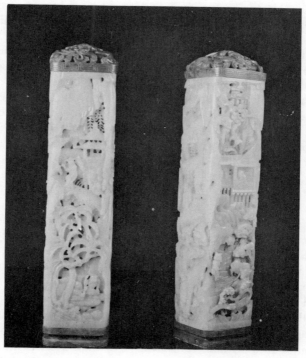

Incense stick holders, sometimes erroneously identified as cricket cages. White, with tops and bottoms of dark green nephrite. H: 10″. W: 2″. 18th or 19th century. Courtesy M. H. De Young Memorial Museum, San Francisco, California. Avery Brundage collection.

Jade, the stone of immortality—an ancient myth or a modern actuality?

One pauses before answering this question, for in our own times jade has successfully survived wars, revolutions, edicts, communes, even an attempt to eradicate the traditional craft of the jade artisan.

We do not have to search the past of jade to find instances of its power and potency. Jade is as remarkable today as it ever was; anew it has proved it possesses that unusual strength which brought its first discoverer to his knees in reverent wonder.

There is a freer, less restrained treatment in many of the carvings of this period . . . Plant motif. White nephrite. H: 5". 18th or 19th century. Courtesy M. H. De Young Memorial Museum, San Francisco, California. Avery Brundage collection.

It is possible that many of the jades classified as Ch'ien Lung were carved long after the Emperor died . . . Vase of almost translucent white nephrite. H: 10". W: 3½". 18th or 19th century. Courtesy M. H. De Young Memorial Museum, San Francisco, California. Avery Brundage collection.

MODERN JADE: FROM CH'IEN LUNG TO MAO TSE-TUNG

The dawn of the modern period of jade occurred in the eighteenth century, during the reign of the Emperor Ch'ien Lung, as major emphasis gradually shifted from the traditional to the decorative aspects of jade. If this period has reached its peak, it has done so in the twentieth century, with the realization of the full potentialities of jadeite by the Chinese and the discovery and great demand for jade by the West.

Yet this period has also contained some of jade's darkest hours; despite the upsurge of world interest in the stone and obvious signs of revitalization within the craft, at least twice the art has come close to extinction.

The Heritage of Ch'ien Lung, 1796–1900

The jade artisans who worked in the studios of the Emperor Ch'ien Lung attained almost unbelievable artistic and technical heights in their carving of jade. Apparently the great creative stimulus given the industry by this extravagant ruler lasted well into the nineteenth century, through the reign of Tao Kuang (1821–50). There is a freer, less restrained treatment in many of the carvings attributed to this later period, most noticeable in the relaxed animal figures. Craftsmen also began experimenting with the use of the "skin" or rind as a part of the finished carving. Still others were making personal adornments and perhaps a few small ornaments of jadeite. It is not only possible but probable that at least some of the jades classified as Ch'ien Lung period were carved during these years, long after Ch'ien Lung had died.

The Emperor's Seal

This is the seal of the Emperor Ch'ien Lung.

Seal of the Emperor Ch'ien Lung (1736–95).

By law it should have been destroyed at the end of his reign. Though the penalty for possessing or duplicating an outdated seal was death, the great demand for the distinctive late-eighteenth-century objects in bronze, porcelain, and jade was sufficient incentive to persuade more than a few artists to tempt fate. There are probably more fraudulent "copies" of the jades of the reign of Ch'ien Lung than of any other period.

Yet let us note what goes into the making of a good "copy" in jade. First, the stone itself must be of quality comparable to the original. Next, the same techniques must be utilized, the same abrasives used, the same amount of time spent in carving. The result may be a fine carving, of Ch'ien Lung *style,* which may pass for a jade of this period.

But again, the weight of the object's value rests on the individual stone and its carving. If purchased and appreciated because it is superb in material and in the skill of the lapidary, there should be no reason for disappointment if one later learns the exact date of its conception. Some of these "copies," of course, were made by the same craftsmen who carved in the studios of Ch'ien Lung.

Most twentieth-century "Ch'ien Lung" jades are another matter altogether. Usually they are readily identifiable, for they have the raw edges and uneven texture that denote the use of the new abrasive, carborundum.

The Boxer Rebellion: End of an Era

During the last half of the nineteenth century the major nephrite carving was in the traditional fields of religious, ceremonial, and funerary objects; in jadeite, as we have already discovered, the chief effort was in the field of jewelry or objects of personal adornment.

The Boxer Rebellion of 1900 marked the end of an era for jade.

The shift to the decorative side of jade became the direction of the art . . . Flower, of light green nephrite. H: 3″. W: 7½″. 20th century. Courtesy M. H. De Young Memorial Museum, San Francisco, California. Avery Brundage collection.

During the last half of the nineteenth century, the major nephrite carving was in traditional fields . . . Vase. White nephrite. H: 10½″. 19th century. Courtesy M. H. De Young Memorial Museum, San Francisco, California. Avery Brundage collection.

For at least two thousand years (probably far longer) jade had been the official stone of the court, its patrons the nobility or the Emperor himself. Most of its major carvings had been created for use by the Imperial family or the state. In 1900 this suddenly changed.

The Boxer Rebellion, aimed at driving foreigners from China, had exactly the opposite effect. They arrived in unprecedented numbers. The influx of Europeans into Peking had a tremendous impact on the jade industry. Here were new buyers with taste entirely different from that of the Chinese, who had revered and admired the simple ancient forms, the sculptures that grew from the rocks themselves, the strong vase and bowl jades. The shift to the decorative side of jade, a gradual movement during the time of Ch'ien Lung, now became *the* direction of the art. The problem of the jade craftsmen was not the absence of Imperial patrons but the scarcity of the stone itself with which to meet the great and sudden demand.

THE WEST'S DISCOVERY OF JADE

It is hoped that the reader will be indulgent when this portion of the narrative occasionally takes on a semi-personal slant.

The Western world has been artistically aware of jade for less than fifty years. Only during the past thirty years has there been an extensive jade trade in the United States. Many of the exciting events which transpired during this period were witnessed firsthand by either the owners or buyers of the firm which I presently head. Their spirited narratives impel me to relate this portion of jade's story just as it happened. In short, this is not a "commercial," but a chronology of some of the liveliest and most important years in the history of jade.

Looking West to the East

Early on the morning of April 18, 1906, an earthquake shook the city of San Francisco from its slumber. It was soon followed by the most destructive fire any American city had ever known. When it ended four days later, the cosmopolitan city seemed to be no more.

GUMP's had at that time been in business forty-five years, since 1861. Under its founder, my grandfather, Solomon Gump, the firm sold mirrors to gold-rush saloons (often repeatedly) and European works of art to the culture-hungry *nouveau riche*. On the morning of the earthquake my father, A. Livingston (or A.L.) Gump and his two brothers were managing the firm. By the end of the second day there was nothing left to manage.

Yet, almost incomprehensible to us now, these were fresh visionary days, bright with optimism. And they mark the beginning of GUMP's interest in the Orient. For while two of the brothers believed in restricting the firm's new merchandise to objects of proven worth, A. L. Gump had glimpsed the unbelievable beauty of the Pacific arts. After months of discussion and argument, a compromise was reached: two thirds of the store would remain devoted to European imports, one third to an Oriental Room.

There was no talk of jade or a Jade Room. People were just beginning to discover the wealth of Japanese art and, in an even more limited sense, Chinese art, but few had ever heard of jade. (Yet perhaps the West's discovery of jade became inevitable the moment the city of San Francisco added the phoenix to its crest.)

Both A. L. Gump and Daniel E. Newell, the firm's first buyer of Oriental goods, were familiar with the stone. They had seen a bit of it in the shops of San Francisco's Chinatown. "In some of the side streets were Chinese jewelers," Newell recollected, "who mounted jade in almost pure gold. Often the rings were elaborately carved. But these were made entirely for the Chinese trade. I can't recall a single Westerner wearing a jade ring before 1920." If there were large jade carvings, they were rarely shown to Occidentals.

A notable exception was the great photographer Arnold Genthe, whose remarkable pictures of San Francisco's Chinatown are a rare visual record of that city within a city as it existed before the great fire. In his autobiography, *As I Remember,* Genthe writes:

> My excursions to Chinatown were not, however, confined entirely to the darker spots. Often my camera was focused on the temple, or Joss House, with its finely wrought gilt carvings dimmed by the smoke of incense, the grotesque divinities of pewter, bronze or porcelain, and the blackened chimney into the mouth of which all papers in Chinese lettering—scraps, posters, handbills, newspapers—were daily consigned by the official paper-gatherer lest they should be defiled by alien feet. A goad to my collector's instinct was the pawnbrokers' and other small shops where discoveries were to be made. Two of my rarest pieces of archaic jade were found in just such places.

Unfortunately, unlike his Chinatown photographs, Genthe's jade collection, one of the earliest in this country, did not survive the fire.

The Oriental department of GUMP's was an immediate success—demand for fine porcelains, paintings, kimonos, embroidered brocades, lacquer, and teakwood often exceeded the supply, though soldiers and marines returning from China after the Boxer Rebellion provided an unexpected source of Asian art—but neither GUMP's nor any of the other Occidental stores stocked jade. There was

Large screen, with gold painting on dark gray-green nephrite. Small panels
H: 7¼". W: 11". Large panels H: 15". W: 11". Total H: 72". 20th century.
Courtesy M. H. De Young Memorial Museum, San Francisco, California.
Avery Brundage collection.

probably very little in America at this time, excluding the China-
towns of New York and San Francisco and individual pieces in a
few museums. Genthe's collection was a rare exception.

On Newell's first trip to Canton in 1907 he visited Jade Street,
center of the jadeite trade in China, "but I didn't buy a single piece,
as I thought there would be no interest in jade at home." On his
second trip, the following year, he visited Shanghai, and there in

one of the shops was shown a small string of graduated jadeite beads. "I inquired the price, which they quoted at 2000 taels, equivalent to $1400 gold! I couldn't believe it! *At home we would have had trouble selling the string for $50!*"

It was not in China but in Japan that Newell finally fell captive to the lure of jade. While shopping for Japanese lacquers in a small shop which usually dealt only with collectors, Newell was promised a very special treat.

The owner brought out two very old boxes and with elaborate care opened the first.

In Newell's own words: "He took out a magnificent white jade vase, carved in the design of the old bronzes of the pre-Christian Era. The carving was superb. In vulgar language, my eyes popped out. *I hadn't known that such pieces existed.* Never had I seen anything like this in China! The second surprise was a vase equally lovely and superbly cut. I asked the prices and was staggered at the answer. *They were priced at several thousand dollars each!*

"Could GUMP's ever sell such pieces when so little was known about jade? I was entranced, yet sure that if I bought them at such a price GUMP's would think me insane and look for a new buyer."

Newell hesitated, thought, looked again at the vases, then weakened and fell victim to what was in time to be one of the occupational diseases of Oriental buyers; my father called it "jade madness," but he did so affectionately, for he too suffered from it.

The two vases had been a gift from the Emperor Ch'ien Lung to the Shogun of Japan in the eighteenth century. As Newell was leaving the shop the owner commented sadly: "How times have changed! This morning I saw the last descendant of the Shogun peddling down the street on a bicycle."

And this afternoon, the dealer was probably thinking, I have seen two of the finest vases ever carved in jade purchased by an American!

Times *had* changed. Though Newell soon returned to China "to seek in every nook and corner of Peking for equally fine jades" and, finding none, "presumed that they were held in the Imperial City by the Empress Dowager or the Manchu princes," jade, the stone of royalty, was now well on its way to becoming the stone of the world. Palace servants, officials, and eunuchs of the falling Manchu line were stealing individual pieces from the royal treasures

A superbly carved, and very rare, complete jade altar set. This Imperial set
came onto the market following the looting of the Summer Palace outside
Peking in 1860. Exceptionally fine dark green nephrite. Vases H: 13¼".
Candlesticks H: 14½". Censer H: 15". w at handles: 10¾". Courtesy
Lizzadro Museum of Lapidary Arts, Elmhurst, Illinois. Mr. and Mrs. Joseph
F. Lizzadro collection.

and selling them to interested parties. Many of these made their
way into private Chinese collections. Few were shown to Westerners, for of course they did not appreciate jade.

Newell's worry over his purchase of the two vases disappeared
the moment A. L. Gump saw them. "He was just as enthusiastic as
I was," Newell related. "I think this single purchase gave us both
an insight into what the future might hold for fine jade."

It also provided the inspiration for GUMP's famed Jade Room.

The Jade Room

To celebrate San Francisco's rebirth and the completion of the
Panama Canal, civic leaders had begun planning, as early as 1910,
the Panama-Pacific International Exposition, to be held in 1915.
It was to be the city's greatest celebration, attracting visitors from
all parts of the world. GUMP's chose this time to expand their own
premises.

Six rooms were to be devoted to the Oriental department. "It seemed wiser to devote more space to the Japanese things than to the little-known Chinese arts," Newell recalled, "but we decided that Chinese art would come into its own in the long run. So we devoted two rooms to Japanese and four to Chinese art. We guessed right, but none of us had any conception of the place Chinese art would soon take in the fine arts."

Nor was the reception of jade foreseen. "We had a little space left which we decided to call the Jade Room," Newell noted in his reminiscences.

Gustave Liljestrom designed the Jade Room. It was high-ceilinged, with only space enough for one large table and four chairs in the center. Along three walls, deep recessed showcases held the precious jades behind walnut doors wrought in Chinese design. Through this room over the coming years would pass thousands of visitors, including many of the world's most noted jade collectors. On display here would be an ever-changing collection of the finest examples of the jade carver's art, at times exceeding a million dollars in value. But, equally important, here uncounted numbers of people would for the first time awaken to jade and vow to possess someday "a piece of Heaven."

But in 1912, when the room was completed, there was not enough jade to fill it. Events were occurring in China at this time, however, which would soon bring to the room jades of great beauty and superb carving that neither A.L. nor Newell dreamed existed.

The Fall of the Ch'ing Dynasty

"The Manchu princes knew they were through," notes Newell, who was in China shortly after the revolution of 1911, "and they took all they could from the Imperial City." Many fine jades appeared on the open market, but in no proportion to the number which were missing from the Imperial treasures.

For years these missing pieces were one of the mysteries of jade, at least as far as American dealers were concerned. Newell accidentally stumbled upon the answer while on a trip to New York in 1912, though it was years before he was certain his suppositions were correct.

Wandering along a cross street near Fifth Avenue, he noticed a shop that carried both Chinese and Japanese goods. It was small but in exquisite taste. Newell conversed at length with the

Many fine jades were missing from the Imperial collection . . . One of a pair of scent boxes, carved in an openwork design, that was at least deserving of a place among the Palace treasures. Greenish-gray nephrite. D: 4⅛″. 18th century or earlier. Courtesy Seattle Art Museum, Seattle, Washington. Eugene Fuller collection.

proprietor, whose home town on the west coast of Japan was known to him. Finally the man brought out his treasures, packed, as was the custom, in old boxes. Last "he brought out a beautiful large green nephrite incense burner about 15 inches high with remarkable pierced carving. It was certainly an Imperial Ch'ien Lung piece. 'Where did you get it?' I asked. 'England,' he replied."

Newell, knowing that a noted jade collector was in New York at the time, asked the merchant if he might show him the piece. The dealer agreed, and Newell took the jade with him, without even being asked for a receipt. The collector bought it on sight. The price was in the neighborhood of $10,000.

While in New York, Newell also called on a Wall Street broker who had ordered a white jade censer sent to him on approval from San Francisco. Its price was $7500, and Newell called to see if he couldn't clinch the sale. He was invited to dinner at the broker's home on Staten Island. Here Newell saw "a collection of jade which took my breath away. Every piece he had was a gem, both as to color and design. I saw the Imperial collection the following year in the Palace at Peking and it didn't compare with his. I suppose some of the New York dealers knew about his collection, but I had never heard that such an outstanding group of jade existed in this country. He had been collecting only a few years."

Newell guessed correctly that when China's last dynasty fell, many of the best of the missing jades "never saw the light of the open market" but were purchased by European dealers, who obviously were ahead of the Americans when it came to discovering jade. The presence of such a collection in New York in 1912 indicates that many of the finest Imperial jades left the Palace long before the revolution. In 1936, when the Imperial collection was moved from Peking to Shanghai to avoid seizure by the Japanese, the disappearing act was duplicated, and a large number of the royal jades mysteriously appeared in the shop of a dealer in Paris.

These, of course, were not the only jades available in the wake of the first revolution. Many Chinese collectors and dealers were also anxious to dispose of their larger jades. Often the old nephrite pieces would be sold to buy perfect cabochons of emerald-green jadeite, easy to hide and of great value.

The beauty and worth of ancient jade were still unappreciated by most of the world, including many of the early jade collectors. C. T. Loo, a noted Oriental art dealer, recalled that in 1914 he purchased a now famous white jade plaque, carved in the form of a tiger, of the Han Dynasty, and sold it for $64. In that same year three-color Chinese porcelains, such as black hawthorns, were bringing from $25,000 to $50,000.

Many Chinese collectors and dealers were anxious to dispose of their larger jades . . . Vase in an archaic bronze form. White nephrite. H: 8¼″. Inscribed with a poem by the Emperor Ch'ien Lung that dates the piece 1773. Courtesy Seattle Art Museum, Seattle, Washington. Eugene Fuller collection.

The Exposition

The Panama-Pacific Exposition of 1915 was a greater success than anyone had imagined, despite the war. During the year of the fair the visitors packed San Francisco, many for the first time to discover the wonders of Asian art. A good many included the Oriental department of GUMP's in their tour and passed through the Jade Room. Few had ever heard of jade before; fewer still had ever handled it or knew that it was more than one of China's "minor arts"; but now, thanks to pieces such as the two Ch'ien Lung vases Newell had brought from Japan, its fame was spreading.

Jade Buying in China

A. L. Gump made his first trip to China in 1917, accompanied by Newell. His own natural intuition, coupled with Newell's experienced guidance, quickly taught him many of the secrets of the trade.

He learned to carry a small piece of jade of known quality, against which other jades could be compared. He learned to bid low and then argue. Though the temptation to make a high bid for some exceptional object was often strong, he discovered that both he and the Chinese must "save face" through protracted bargaining. From his long experience with the merchants of San Francisco's Chinatown, he knew that often a potential buyer would be "tested" by first being shown inferior merchandise, that if his choice was wrong he would never see the real treasures, which would be held for the more discriminating. When on a buying trip he learned to wear his oldest clothes, because one Chinese frankly told him, "Mr. Gump, you look too much rich." It was harder to learn to disguise his natural joy upon examining a beautiful object. The Chinese were aware that the pupils of the eyes dilated when one's interest was aroused, and acted accordingly. Newell had earlier solved this problem by wearing dark glasses.

When the two reached Shanghai, A.L. learned a great deal more about the Chinese jade trade from one of the most important men in the business, his *comprador.*

The Comprador

The comprador might be described as the Chinese middleman in jade, though his function is often both more complex and subtle. It is his job to bring together the buyer and the seller, with commissions from both sides. Sometimes he will himself purchase the objects, then resell them, since some merchants have two prices—one for foreigners, another for Chinese.

For many years GUMP's comprador in China was a man named Liu. Liu possessed a rigid but almost incomprehensible set of business ethics. On one occasion he mortgaged his home and most of his possessions to place a higher bid than A.L. had indicated, in order that A.L. might not lose face; yet a few days later he argued for hours with A.L. over a few dollars in a minor transaction.

Pigeons and Jade

Early in this friendship, A.L. found Liu selling "jade" jewelry, manufactured in Germany, to some visiting tourists.

"It's bad business to cheat your patrons that way," A.L. commented.

"No matter," Liu philosophized. "One-time pigeon, never see again."

"I wouldn't like to have you treat me that way," A.L. persisted.

Liu's face lit up. "Ah, no," he exclaimed, "you all-time pigeon!"

A good comprador had to know the pulse of China. He had to be aware when exceptionally fine merchandise was being offered

The Chinese were aware that the pupils of the eyes dilated when one's interest was aroused . . . Peony bowl. White nephrite. H: 2 11/16". D: 6⅜". Courtesy Seattle Art Museum, Seattle, Washington. Eugene Fuller collection.

for sale, either by individuals or syndicates, in whatever part of the country, and be able to act quickly on this knowledge. Liu was such a comprador, with seemingly unlimited sources of information, as A.L. discovered. Once after A.L. and Newell had made a short trip to Shanghai, they met Liu again in Peking.

"See these," Liu said, indicating a stack of letters, easily three inches thick, on his desk. "These all about you, everything you do in Shanghai."

"Who are they from?" A.L. asked, amazed.

"My friends," Liu replied. "They know you my friend, so they write all about you."

There is no such thing as secrecy in China, especially when one is on a "jade hunt."

Jade Hunting

On his trip in 1917, A.L. bought brocades, bronzes, Imperial rugs, Korean amber, teakwood, paintings, and scrolls—but his greatest interest was jade. This was his first jade hunt, and he collected impressions, knowledge, and the stone itself avidly.

In Canton, with its seven jade houses, he learned the range and value of jewel jade, or jadeite. He felt the raw stone, newly arrived from the remote mountains of Burma, watched its sale on the open market, and observed the craftsmen at work in the shops, turning it into beads, pendants, and rings. He examined and purchased brilliant emerald-green cabochons and strings of jadeite beads, aware of the artistic value of jadeite, but not dreaming that within a few years a perfect necklace of these beads would sell for a reputed $100,000 to a great heiress.

In Peking he was in the midst of the nephrite trade and, through the mysterious connections of Liu, encountered many of the older jades, which were now slowly making their way from family collections into the hands of jade merchants and syndicates. He saw and bought several Ch'ien Lung pieces. One, an ornament measuring 2 by 1½ inches, was as thin as parchment; yet on one side, in a lace-like effect, were carved peonies, butterflies, and birds, while the opposite side bore a scroll with the Buddhist unending knot of happiness.

He missed no chance to feel the jades he was shown, the few superior and the many inferior objects, as if storing up impressions

Many of the older jades were mysteriously making their way into the hands
of jade merchants and syndicates . . . White nephrite vase, based on a
bronze form. H: 9″. D: 6¾″. 18th century. Courtesy M. H. De Young
Memorial Museum, San Francisco, California. Avery Brundage collection.

and cultivating the tactile sense which would soon have to replace
his sight.

The Ch'ien Lung Jades

Before leaving China, A.L. told Liu to cable him immediately
if any other Ch'ien Lung jades became available. In 1919 Liu
learned that one of the largest and most important groups of Ch'ien
Lung jades yet discovered was in the hands of a Chinese syndicate.
A.L. authorized Joe Wheeler, the new Far Eastern buyer, to stay
in China until this superb collection of Imperial vases, jars, bowls,
and wine pots could be obtained for the right price. Wheeler
stayed three years.

A.L. followed every phase of the negotiations, refusing to

give up hope when they reached apparent stalemates. The syndicate had infinite patience, but their time was running out, A.L. realized, as he watched reports of the northward progress of the Chinese People's Army. Then in 1922, when word came that the army had sacked Nanking, A.L. played his trump card, cabling a final offer, the lowest he had yet made.

Aware that the syndicate would rather have an easily concealed draft on an American bank than the bulky jade jars, which stood several feet high, A.L. gambled and won. The collection became the property of GUMP'S.

Several Ch'ien Lung jades, previously offered for sale, were not in the final consignment. Agents were commissioned to scour China for them. Only one was ever found. Sixteen years later Martin Rosenblatt, then the store's buyer, was in the jade market in Peking when a small boy passed carrying one of the missing jades, which Rosenblatt identified by its distinctive graining and color. The boy would not reveal where his master had obtained it, and the others were never found.

It was these, the jades of the Emperor Ch'ien Lung, that made the Jade Room famous and established A. L. Gump's world-wide reputation as a buyer of jade.

The Jade Rush

The era was the 1920s. A decade earlier few people had heard of jade. Now the whole world seemed aware of it. Ten, twenty-five, fifty thousand dollars; these were not unusual prices for a fine Ch'ien Lung vase. A bird cage with jade cups brought $1200 in a New York auction. Women were discovering that jade jewelry enhanced the natural beauty of their skin. As was to be the case in the years that followed, demand far exceeded supply. Buyers from all countries crowded Peking, Canton, and Shanghai. And more and more tourists, in both China and Japan, sought jade in preference to cloisonné, ivory, and pearls. All this had a marked effect on the jade industry itself.

In the jade shops of Canton, Wheeler found more than fifteen hundred artists and apprentices employed in fashioning modern pieces, many based on ancient designs, as well as jade jewelry. In Peking alone there were over 300 jade workshops turning out objects of all sizes and qualities, including large elaborate ornaments, the thinly cut Tibetan-style bowls, vases, and censers, as well as Koro tripod-style censers for the Japanese. Hundreds worked at carving small decorative pieces that could be sold to tourists.

Despite the use of the faster abrasives, the constant demand for more objects, and the feverish activity, many really superb objects of almost miraculous craftsmanship were made during these years, almost up to the time of World War II.

Only one thing threatened to upset this boom—the scarcity of fine-quality jade.

Though both nephrite and jadeite were being cut from the hills in greater quantity, neither was of the fine quality of previous years. Jadeite hat tubes, buckles, and thumb rings, some perhaps dating as far back as the time of Ch'ien Lung, were now cut into modern salable pieces. Often a whole object was destroyed to obtain its central jewel spot for a cabochon. If you examine a jade ring you may discover a groove in the back of the jade, indicating it was once a hat tube or the top of a snuff bottle. Or you may find two holes, which betray its original use as a button. Many Mandarin necklaces were cut up. In addition to the 108 uniform beads, there were three larger beads on the string, sometimes cut from excep-

The recutting of old jade to meet new tastes was a brisk business . . . Pair of fluted bowls of translucent white nephrite, probably 18th century, recut into the thin Indian or Tibetan style at a much later date. H: 2½". D: 5¾". Courtesy M. H. De Young Memorial Museum, San Francisco, California. Avery Brundage collection.

tional-quality jadeite. Any one of these, cut in two and used as the gem for a ring, would sell more readily to the Europeans and Americans than the whole string in its original form.

The recutting of old jade to meet new tastes was a brisk business. Martin Rosenblatt had this fact brought home to him graphically. In 1948, while in Peking, he was shown a group of fine eighteenth-century white nephrite bowls and vases. Considering the price too high, he hesitated; several weeks later he returned to make another offer, only to find that the pieces were at that moment in a nearby shop, being ground thinner to make them more translucent and more like Tibetan jades, which were currently more salable.

Liu's Jade

About 1920 a new type of jade came onto the Peking market. It was spinach-green nephrite, unusual in its depth of color and translucency, with specks of black graphite distributed thoughout the stone. It was quite different from the green nephrite previously known. The dealers hesitated to use it. Comprador Liu bought one piece weighing over two tons. When cut, it proved to be of fabulous color, with no flaws and almost no waste.

It is now known that this remarkable stone was found near Sinkiang and brought to China by Russians. From it came some of the finest of the large green jade carvings made prior to World War II. Other dealers followed Liu's lead. There were several tons of additional material, also of fine quality, imported and sold. But then, as always happens, the bonanza was at an end. None of the subsequent jade, obtained from the same source, ever came close to equaling "Liu's jade," as it is now known.

The Darkest Hours

Within the memory of most of us, two events occurred which—probably more than any others in the three-thousand-year history of the jade carver's art—threatened to extinguish this art.

The first was World War II, during which many of the carvers were conscripted for military service, a great number never to return to their benches. The second was the decision of the Chinese Communist government, in 1950, to abolish the craft of jade carving.

Martin Rosenblatt describes most graphically the situation in Peking in 1946, following the war:

An 18th-century bowl of dark green nephrite, also recut at a later date
to conform to the current Western tastes. H: 3¾". D: 11". Courtesy M.
H. De Young Memorial Museum, San Francisco, California. Avery
Brundage collection.

"Where in 1936 and 1938 Jade Street was filled with shops and
merchandise, in 1946 there were only about 18 or 20 jade-working
shops and less than half of the retail shops were still in existence.
The war had depleted materials, especially abrasives. Everywhere
jade merchants said 'No corundum—price corundum very high—
jade costs now very high.' The choice of jades and other hard
stones was extremely disappointing. No one was making jade trees
—no one was even cutting Peking glass. Most of the workers were
forced to seek other work; it was too expensive to house and feed
apprentices."

In 1948 the picture was even darker. It was impossible to obtain
fine jade at any price. One carver has said that in 1949 there were
fewer than 100 jade carvers still working in Peking.

In 1950 the first reports came to Hong Kong of repressive steps
in all crafts. The younger jade carvers were conscripted into the
army; the older men were put to work on farms. The jade industry
was apparently doomed; actually, outside of Hong Kong, it no
longer existed.

Nor did the Communist Chinese government simply halt the
carving of jade. It banned the export of jade, labeling those pieces

which had already been carved "national treasures," forestalling any attempt to ship them out of the country.

For eight long years jade carving knew its darkest hours. True, carvers were at work in Hong Kong and Japan, but their output was small, pitifully inadequate to meet world demand. The Japanese did fine work in jade jewelry, but they seemed unable to master the larger carvings, such as vases and bowls, nor did they have the skill of the Chinese in depicting the human figure.

Jade's Victory

But in 1958 jade again proved itself to be the stone of immortality. Even though the victory was almost purely financial in intent, it was no less a triumph: the Chinese Communist government, needing foreign exchange, realized it had almost extinguished one of its most profitable arts. Back from the farms, out of the communes, they brought the carvers, to re-establish the craft of jade.

Accurate reports from inside China describe the current resurrection of the art.

Jade workshops have been set up in Peking, Canton, Shanghai, Chingchow, Nanyang, Chengchow, Tientsin, Yangchow, Chentu, and Chengping. Here the old artisans teach hundreds of student apprentices their trade. Most of the apprentices are primary and junior middle school graduates in their teens, who are given three years of training, with government subsidies for clothing, board, and lodging. *About half of them are girls!* The advent of electricity late in 1958, replacing the two-foot-pedal-power, has made the work less strenuous. In Peking more than fourteen hundred carvers belong to the Peking Jade Studios and work in a large new four-story building.

And their products?

The shops and lofts of Hong Kong are bulging with them today. Much is tawdry and overelaborate; much is hurried and shows the use of the faster abrasives. But occasionally one discovers a fine piece with that subtle grace where the carving is in exact harmony with the stone. It is interesting what they are carving—figures, animals, and birds, mostly. Mythological or religious figures are rarely seen; history and popular folklore provide many of the subjects. In styles these carvings are much more realistic than those of previous decades. Too, they are not wrought to fit the peculiar shape of the boulder or stone but seem, in most cases, to have been cut from squared blocks of stone. Very few bowls or vases are carved, perhaps because they entail too much labor and require finer raw materials.

These are not the only jades on the Hong Kong market. Objects less than one hundred years old are no longer considered national treasures by the Chinese Communist government, and though most of them are of secondary quality, a really fine piece occasionally slips through, probably unrecognized by the censors. It is reminiscent of Communist Russia in its days of selling jewels of Fabergé and many other objects not considered of national importance.

More and more jewel jade is appearing in Hong Kong. We have been told that if a person in Communist China is known to have a treasure that the censors consider exportable, he receives a visit from an agent, who urges him to sell it to the government. If he refuses, he is visited again, this time by two agents. It is usually not long before "patriotism" compels him to sell his jade at a very modest price.

Americans can look and touch and appreciate these jades from inside China—but they cannot buy them. To import jade into the United States at the present time, one must produce a certificate of origin for each piece. As each Hong Kong craftsman finishes a carving it is registered, and on this basis certificates are made. If the jade comes from inside Communist China, a certificate cannot be obtained.

Fortunately, among the Hong Kong craftsmen are many of the old jade carvers who at one time fled from China proper, and among their carvings are many worthy of appreciation and purchase. But they are still too few.

Perhaps in the not too distant future the picture will again change.

But today, as always, the greatest threat to the art of jade carving is not man and his dictates but the rarity of the stone. Fine-quality Turkestan nephrite and Burmese jadeite are available in far smaller quantities than they were even a dozen years ago. Prices rise steadily, for as the supply diminishes and more of the world learns to appreciate jade, it is becoming even more precious than precious stones.

Head of a Bodhisattva. Green nephrite. H: 29″. Sung Dynasty. Courtesy Seattle Art Museum, Seattle, Washington. Eugene Fuller collection.

CHAPTER TEN

BUYING A "PIECE OF HEAVEN"

. . . and that is why the wise set so great store by jade . . .

Confucius

What should I look for when purchasing jade?
Where can I find fine jade?
What should I pay?

How can I tell if it is real jade?
Are there any rules that would help me?
What are some of the jade frauds?

Are there any bargains in jade?
Can I afford jade?
What's the right jade—for me?

Thousands ask these questions, both silently and vocally. Had there been readily accessible answers following World War II, hundreds of servicemen, travelers, and tourists returning from the Orient would not have had to be told that their bargain jade purchases in China and Japan were green glass, serpentine, or jade of inferior quality. As a result, they would now feel a deep personal pleasure rather than resentment at mention of the word.

This chapter contains the answers to these questions, in the form of a number of basic rules for buying quality jade. These rules are little more than applied common sense. Coupled with your own natural intuition, they should enable you, when the occasion arrives, to purchase the jade or jades for you, without second thoughts and regrets.

TRUE AND PSEUDO JADE

Long ago a wit coined a now classic maxim: DEMAND CREATES SUPPLY. This is, unfortunately, particularly apropos of jade.

Before noting some of the major frauds in jade, let's mention a few ways in which the buyer may be "honestly" deceived.

Is It Yü? The Price of a Single Word

Remembering that the Chinese have always been somewhat loose in their use of the term *yü*, often using it to refer to any stone of great beauty, we should not be surprised that even today there are merchants in Hong Kong who do not clearly elucidate the nature of the stone they are selling. Nor is this habit confined to this British crown colony. There are merchants in almost every country who have the same semantic difficulties.

They may speak of an object as being jasper jade (which is jasper), colored jade (which is dyed jade), pink jade (which is dyed quartz), Mexican jade (dyed onyx), or India jade (a name often given to aventurine, a green quartz with particles of mica in it, a stone that on first glance often looks like jade but bears a much lower price tag). Or they may simply mention that an object is Soochow jade, knowing that the name alone will conjure up the romantic image of a fabled Oriental city. And they are being semi-honest; it is manufactured in the city of Soochow. But it isn't jade; it is a hard, compact form of serpentine, highly similar in appearance and texture to nephrite, worked by the same methods, occasionally radiating nearly the same colors. It is carved not so much to pass for jade as to fill the demand of Chinese buyers who want carvings yet cannot afford them in jade.

Further semantic difficulties may arise in the interpretation of the term *Han jade*, which does not mean that the object was carved in the Han Dynasty, but that—like Han Dynasty jades—it was a burial jade, one preserved in the tombs. *Imperial jade*, too, is confusing. To the Chinese merchant it does not mean that the particular jade was once in the Imperial collection, but rather that it appears fit for Imperial use (is of top quality), remarkable for the excellence of both the stone and its carving.

Similar to . . .

A number of stones resemble or may be made to resemble jade. Serpentine is perhaps the most common; soapstone runs a close second. Even glass and plastics have on occasion been marketed as jade. Other materials, such as californite and amazonite, even closer in appearance to nephrite or jadeite, are not, fortunately, native to the Celestial Kingdom, therefore only rarely pose as jade.

Glass, soapstone, and plastics can be scratched with a penknife; real jade cannot, except, of course, archaic or tomb jades which may have undergone chemical alteration. Some of these will even powder slightly when handled.

When it comes to jewelry, glass beads (of all colors, common in China) are frequently mistaken for jadeite. Glass under a strong magnifying glass can usually be recognized by its air bubbles. To determine whether beads are of glass or jade, examine the holes at the ends; jade will be polished, glass will be sharp and will often be chipped, the chips having a concave or shell-like shape.

There is no simple method by which to determine whether you are being shown jade or one of its substitutes. You must learn by study and experience, just as a diamond expert learns his profession. Jade feels cold, smooth, and hard to the touch, but so do many other stones that look like it. Some imitations, like soapstone, quickly absorb the warmth of the hand and feel uneven or soft. In some cases you may scratch them with your fingernail. A small jade sample often makes a better scratch piece, but remember, there are many stones as hard as jade.

Often only chemical analysis will determine whether a suspect piece is real jade or a similar material. Even dealers are sometimes fooled. Knowing this, you might wonder how anyone could ever buy the stone with assurance. There is a simple answer, which is also your first and most important rule in jade buying.

1. BUY ONLY FROM A REPUTABLE MERCHANT.

It is his business to make sure that the product he offers is what he claims. His reputation depends on it. Many dealers will go to the expense of having a piece tested if there is the slightest doubt regarding its composition. Moreover, putting these considerations aside and assuming that someone makes a mistake, with a reputable firm you have redress.

The obvious next question (mentioned at the risk of alienating many) is: Where does one find a reputable merchant?

In Hong Kong: To obtain a list of reputable shops, check with

Servicemen's Guides (which maintains a booth at Fenwick Pier), the American Express Company, or the American Embassy. Most of the large department stores also stock jade, usually at prices higher than in the native shops. Don't hire a native guide; his commission will be added to what you ordinarily would have paid. Avoid the advice of well-meaning friends ("Let me give you the address of the cutest little jade shop in Hong Kong . . .") unless you are quite sure they know jade.

There are a number of excellent jade shops in Hong Kong. There are also those where you are considered a "one-time pigeon" and whose philosophy is: "If he's happy with a fake, why give him the real thing?" If you choose an honest firm at the outset, you'll probably pay more, but you'll be buying real jade.

In the United States: Buy from a store with an established reputation. If you are personally unfamiliar with the firm, check with someone who knows it. You are making an investment when you buy jade, therefore you should eliminate all possible risk.

If you stick to this first and most important rule, you will eliminate most of your jade-buying problems.

There will be occasions when you might wish to disregard it. Perhaps in a streetside bazaar you will find an attractive string of beads you'd like to own that looks like jade. Or an odd carving. Or again, in an American store, an attractive pin or pendant that the salesgirl thinks is jade. If you like it, buy it, but only because you like it for what it is. Don't pay the price of jade unless you are sure it *is* jade.

2. BEFORE YOU BUY, GET ACQUAINTED WITH THE STONE.

If at all possible, before you make your first purchase of jade, visit one or more museums with jade collections and observe the craftsmanship and beauty of the pieces on display. A list of the most prominent collections open to public view is included following this chapter. But don't restrict your viewing to museums. Visit several stores that sell jade. Handle the pieces that interest you. To really appreciate jade, you must feel as well as see it.

Don't stop with one or two stores; you'll miss half the fun of buying. The excitement of jade hunting is not limited to China; you'll know it when you begin seeking the right jades for you.

Before discussing things to look for when jade shopping, let's mention a few more "jades" to avoid.

NOTABLE JADE FRAUDS

Dyed Jade Jewelry

Not too many years ago a well-dressed Chinese gentleman took a jade bracelet into a Hong Kong pawnshop. The bracelet was made of high-carat gold, each piece of jade mounted separately in a heavy frame.

The proprietor knew jade, having had many years of experience in handling it. He examined the stones carefully, establishing to his own satisfaction that they were of very fine emerald-green jadeite. And so he lent the man a considerable amount of money on the bracelet; of course the amount was by no means proportionate to the bracelet's apparent worth.

When several months had passed and the man did not return to claim his pawn, the proprietor examined it more carefully. On removing the stones from their setting, he found that, though they were indeed jade, they were dyed doublets. Dyed jade had been fitted inside a shell of colorless transparent jade; another piece of transparent jade had been fitted across the bottom of the shell. The finished piece was then set in a heavy frame to conceal the joints.

The repercussions were felt around the world.

In Europe, America, and all parts of the Orient, merchants and private collectors hurriedly examined their jade cabochons. More than a few discovered they had been swindled. Most of the frauds were simply dyed—without benefit of the doublet casing.

In New York a dealer placed an expensive green jade ring in his window display. Two weeks later, when he removed it, it had faded to a sickly yellow green, the dye having been affected by the sunlight.

On the West Coast, a woman brought a gold set, mounted with beautiful emerald-green stones, into the jewelry department of our store in hopes of finding a ring to match. Unfortunately the jades had an unusual tone or color, what an appraiser would call a "synthetic look." Under a ten-power glass, dyed areas were revealed, strange threadlike lines of color. As is usually the case, white jadeite had been used for the dye treatment. Jadeite, as we have already noted, is *microcrystalline;* the minute crystalline crevices are where the dye takes hold. Fortunately the story had a reasonably happy ending. The dealer who had sold her the set, genuinely shocked, made restitution.

During 1957 more than 25,000 pieces of dyed jade are known to have been imported into the United States. One enterprising pusher made $10,000 on the sale of a single small consignment to an eastern jeweler, who should have suspected his marvelous bargain.

To keep within the Federal Trade Commission's regulations, the producers of this product made sure it was labeled "dyed jade" when it passed through customs. Some dealers were not so explicit when the jade was sold to the customers.

Before long, customs officials detected a new reverse twist to the problem: some of the Chinese exporters were including real, fine jade in "dyed jade" shipments to their agents, to take advantage of the much lower duty on the bogus product.

Happily, once attention was focused on the fraud, many of the producers of dyed jade sought other fields for their creative endeavors. Very little dyed jade has appeared on the market during the past several years. Again, your safeguard is to buy only from reputable dealers. Dyed jade is also sometimes labeled "colored" or "treated" jade.

Jade Copies

Now to the carvings. Most copies of ancient jades, many themselves ancient in origin, were not originally carved with intent to deceive or defraud, but merely to re-create a respected traditional form. Sometimes even these may assume value, as have many of the copies made during the Sung period.

One important factor that has kept outright frauds at a minimum has already been mentioned: to reproduce an ancient piece, you must use the same time-consuming techniques. The patina on buried jades may be simulated, but sharp edges, hurried workmanship, and uneven finish quickly disclose modern methods of carving. The older carvings in nephrite have a more unctuous quality.

Liu once commented on another feature of the old carvings: "The fine old antiques have a fresh, sharp quality to them, despite breakage, wearing, handling. Each piece has a briskness and a vigor. You can almost say they look *new,* while the frauds are generally dirtied up, rubbed and worn away in strange places, made to look old."

There are fraudulent carvings on the market, but if you follow the first rule of jade buying there is little chance you'll ever have one in your own collection.

BUYING ANTIQUE JADE

In foregoing chapters we have already mentioned some of the difficulties in dating. To summarize these:

To be absolutely sure of an object's age, it must be obtained from a scientifically excavated tomb. Few such jades are on the market. Many from the looted tombs are, and these must be judged against the dated jades or parallels in other art forms of the period.

Over the centuries there are different periods of design and style in the carving. (See Chapter Five: "The Jade Dynasties.") The style or design of an object would, generally speaking, indicate the period. For example, there are many designs in use at present which did not exist seventy-five years ago.

Is the piece original or an imaginative copy? Check the exact detail of design. If it is a Han vessel (suspect in itself) with a Ming or Sung design, you know something is wrong. During the Victorian age, Europeans copied Gothic furniture, but they would introduce into the design elements unknown in Gothic times. It is the same with jade. Look for anachronisms.

The material that is used is also a good indicator. If the piece is said to be pre-1784 and of jadeite, look out. If it is labeled Ch'ien Lung and of the distinctive spinach-green Russian jade of Liu, which came onto the market in 1920, you would again have due cause for suspicion.

Does the piece have raw edges or uneven texture? Do the cross lines or the fine engraved designs have loose ends, or do they cut across each other? Then beware. The antique jades were made as ritual objects for divine forces which the Chinese believed could see all. They had to be perfect. Time was not as pressing in those days, and the slower cutting abrasives were more readily controlled. The same is true of the antique cameos and intaglios of Rome. The ancient ones are marvels of perfection. The frauds are faulty and crude by comparison.

There will be borderline cases, which is all the more reason that you should rely on the discrimination and experience of a reputable merchant when buying any kind of jade, but especially antique jade.

3. IN BUYING AN ANTIQUE, BE PREPARED TO SPEND TIME IN ESTAB-
LISHING ITS AUTHENTICITY.

Just because an object is old does not make it good. However,
if you are buying a certain jade because of its age, you must be
merciless in tracking it down, thoroughly scholarly in your
approach. If your sole consideration is the beauty of the carving,
you can afford to be less exact. If age is uppermost to you, be
prepared to spend both time and money in obtaining expert
guidance.

It cannot be overstressed that some of the finest ar'd most
beautiful jades ever carved are products of our own century.
Don't be misled by age—it is the quality of the stone and its
carving that counts.

GENERAL RULES FOR JUDGING AND BUYING FINE JADE

4. BUY JADE ONLY AFTER HAVING SEEN IT UNDER NATURAL LIGHT.
This rule applies to both carving and jewelry.

North light is best; sunlight will do; but artificial light intensifies
the green. An object may look exceedingly glamorous in a showcase,
with appropriate background, but only natural light will reveal
the blemishes and the true color of the stone. The clerk who
appreciates fine jade will be glad to oblige you; it will give him or
her an equally pleasurable opportunity to see the color of the stone
at its best.

5. TO JUDGE QUALITY AND COLOR, USE ANOTHER PIECE OF ESTAB-
LISHED MERIT FOR COMPARISON.

The man whose business it is to purchase jade will either wear or
carry one or more quality pieces, often one of nephrite and another
of jadeite. The collector of jade could do no better than buy a
small fondling piece, which can be used for both judging jade
and elevating the thoughts. Few women have to be persuaded to
wear jewel jade or jadeite, "because jade is the most sumptuous
jewel against a woman's flesh . . ."

What to Look For

You have already observed the great variance in the quality of
different pieces. A large censer several feet in height, if of poor

material or workmanship, may be worth less, both financially and artistically, than a palm-size snuff bottle of perfect color.

The fact that an object is of jade does not make it good, nor does it automatically confer unusual value. For jade to have value *to you*, you must be satisfied on three important points.

6. WHEN JUDGING A JADE CARVING ASK YOURSELF:
   1. *Is the object of fine material?*
   2. *In workmanship, is it a worthy example of its craft?*
   3. *Do I really appreciate this particular piece?*

The merchant may ignore the last point, though it is certainly unwise to do so. The period collector of jades, if his purchases are based solely on age, may skip all three, though he is not likely to emerge with a very good collection.

But you, if you desire not only to possess but also to enjoy jade, must insist to your own satisfaction on all three.

Let us consider these important points singly.

Material

What do you look for in the stone itself?

First, consistency of color. The color will be a matter of preference. But see that it is consistent to the total carving, that there are no splotches of disquieting hue that detract from the over-all concept.

Look for flaws, fractures, irregularities in the material. Sometimes a crack is filled in with wax; feeling the whole piece and examining it carefully should reveal this.

Workmanship

When examining carved jade, consider both the over-all effect of the carving and the detail. See whether it has delicacy of execution, totally and in part. Observe how the artist has utilized the nature of the stone. Examine it closely. Are the lines distinct and clean, or uneven with occasional overlapping? Feel the whole piece for softness of line. If it is antique jade—Ch'in Lung and earlier—it should have no sharp corners, no raw edges, no matter what the forms utilized by the carver.

Diamonds are valued in carats; gold is valued by weight; paintings are usually valued by the reputation of the artist. A piece of jade can be valued only by its inherent quality. It may be of the

Ming Dynasty; but is it a good carving of fine material? It may stand three feet high, weigh twenty-eight pounds, have been ten years in the carving; but is it a worthy example of its craft?

7. IF IN DOUBT, DON'T BUY.

This is a cardinal rule in purchasing anything. If, after having handled and studied a piece, judging it on its material and workmanship, there remains doubt, then it is not for you. Jade cannot be a casual purchase; you cannot think "it will do" and then expect it to grow in your esteem. Jade is rare, but not so rare that you can't afford to pass up a piece that doesn't totally satisfy you.

These must be your considerations when buying jade. But equally essential is your appreciation. Without it, jade is just another possession, another precious stone. Appreciation in this case is synonymous with getting "the feel" of jade and is applicable to both carved and gem jade.

The Feel of Jade

When the Chinese use this term they mean much more than feeling it in the tactile sense, with the fingers. "Feeling jade," in the Chinese manner, is getting to know it by letting the stone reveal itself to you.

This may sound abstract; it is really very simple and basic. It simply means approaching each carving you view or handle freshly, as if it were in itself something very special, unique.

When you examine jade, look at it as if you were seeing the stone for the very first time. Let it surprise you, as it will. Approach it from different angles. If your main interest is color, for just a moment forget the color and study the carving or the form. Give the stone the chance to excite you. There should be no such thing as being jaded to the buying of jade.

Or to the possessing of it. For, unlike objects chosen with an eye to current fashion trends, a jade carving will never pall; each time you see or handle it you will discover deeper reasons for your appreciation. As any collector will testify, one must live with a piece of jade to appreciate it fully. Jade is a tough stone, it is a rare stone, but one thing it is not: it is not a static stone. Owning, seeing, handling it, you will be amazed how a single piece can so perfectly fit your many moods.

This is a part of what the Chinese mean by the "feel of jade."

The Price of Jade

What should I pay for jade?

To determine the current prices of jade, compare the prices of similar pieces in several stores. Remembering that no two pieces are ever alike, nor will their prices be, you can still get an idea of what you must pay to get the type of jade you desire. Jade prices change, but they go in only one direction, *up*.

You can afford jade; everyone can. Even if your first acquisition is a single piece of jade jewelry or a small fondling piece, which grows ever more beautiful as you handle it, this can be the beginning of your jade collection; with it you can begin to get "the feel." Many like to start with a small but good piece of jade, perhaps a tiny contemporary animal figure, a small dish, or maybe an old snuff bottle. In a Chinese market you will find jade ranging from small broken chips of carvings at a few cents to larger pieces at many dollars, since almost everyone in China wants to own at least one piece of jade.

At present, if you buy outside the United States, the duty on unset stones is 5 per cent, on gold-mounted 30 per cent. There is no duty on jade carved prior to 1830, known as antique jade, but you may have trouble proving the age of the carving. (Especially if customs officials find it is jadeite.)

Must you haggle over price? It depends on the dealer and your relationship with him. In general, in the Orient one should not agree to the first price. After many centuries this still causes everyone concerned to "lose face," and yet today there are some who maintain a one-price standard. You must know the dealer and know the market.

John Goette tells the story of a British merchant in Hong Kong who, on the way to a party, decided to buy a jade bracelet for his hostess. Keeping his cab waiting, he ran into a jade shop he frequently patronized, saw the bracelet he wanted, and agreed to the first price. The Chinese proprietor was horrified and refused to sell him the piece. Only after forcing the money upon him and rushing out to his cab was the Briton able to conclude the sale. For weeks afterward the Chinese, so sure that his customer had noticed something special about the piece that he had missed, moaned to all his dealer friends, "I have been taken!"

8. BE SUSPICIOUS OF UNUSUALLY LOW PRICES.

This is the best indication of an imitation or a jade of inferior quality. I don't know of a single instance of a purchaser outwitting a Chinese merchant on a piece of jade. The Chinese who sell it know their trade; they have a three-thousand-year jump on us, perception to fine jade being almost an inborn part of their nature.

9. REMEMBER, FINE JADE IS BOTH AN ARTISTIC AND A FINANCIAL INVESTMENT.

Are there bargains in jade? Yes, but they come not from unwary merchants but from time.

Any fine jade you buy today, of good material and workmanship, at the prevailing market prices, is a bargain, in terms of what this piece will sell for ten years from now. Jade is an investment which has survived depressions and fluctuating markets to increase in value in the past and will continue to do so in the future.

Once only China was interested in jade; today the whole world is a ready market. Even were Communist China open to world trade and all the jade shops in operation, exporting jade at maximum capacity, there would not be enough *fine* carvings to meet the demand, for not only does the quality of the raw stone seem to be diminishing, but even in jade's best years the superb carving is an exception.

The same holds true in jewelry—it is extremely difficult to obtain fine gem jade.

Nature's bounty is not unlimited. It is inevitable that, as world interest in jade grows, the increasing scarcity of quality stone will in itself drive prices higher and higher.

In the world today there are few investments, either financial, artistic, or aesthetic, as safe and sure and satisfying as the purchase of fine jade.

BASIC RULES FOR BUYING JADE

1. BUY ONLY FROM A REPUTABLE MERCHANT.
2. BEFORE YOU BUY, GET ACQUAINTED WITH THE STONE.
3. IN BUYING AN ANTIQUE, BE PREPARED TO SPEND TIME IN ESTABLISHING ITS AUTHENTICITY.
4. BUY JADE ONLY AFTER HAVING SEEN IT UNDER NATURAL LIGHT.
5. TO JUDGE QUALITY AND COLOR, USE ANOTHER PIECE OF ESTABLISHED MERIT FOR COMPARISON.

6. WHEN JUDGING A JADE CARVING ASK YOURSELF:
   a. Is the object of fine material?
   b. In workmanship, is it a worthy example of its craft?
   c. Do I really appreciate this particular piece?
7. IF IN DOUBT, DON'T BUY.
8. BE SUSPICIOUS OF UNUSUALLY LOW PRICES.
9. REMEMBER, FINE JADE IS BOTH AN ARTISTIC AND A FINANCIAL INVESTMENT.

JADE: A CONCLUSION AND A BEGINNING . . .

For at least three thousand years the stone of Heaven has also been the stone of man. During this time the Chinese not only developed jade carving into one of the world's finest arts, they made the stone the core of their civilization. Even more, they accepted it as a bridge between man as he is and as he can be. In its beauty they caught a glimpse of Heaven, in its handling an awakening to wonder.

Jade is the stone of superlatives as well as the stone of Heaven: The Quintessence of Creation. The Philosopher's Stone. The Timeless Stone. The Stone of Immortality. The Evocative Stone. The Most Sumptuous Jewel. These are only man's attempts, as is this book, to penetrate more deeply to the mystery that lies in the heart of jade.

Yet the mystery remains, as always, a very personal one. And that is as it should be. For the three thousand years of myth, creation, and history are only a prologue to that timeless moment when each of us discovers jade and lets it reveal both its overt and its hidden beauty. Here is the real beginning of the story of jade, when each of us makes the stone his or her own.

There can be no definitive book on jade. There is no last chapter in its story, though several have tried to write it, forgetting that jade is a living stone. It would be relatively easy to conclude, from current perspective, that in view of the scarcity of the raw stone and the fact that China seems to have forgotten jade's meaning, remembering only its commercial value, the future of jade is dark and foreboding.

But, remembering that for more than three thousand years it has never been a common stone, that also during this period it has survived all changing forms of government, the picture is less grim.

As to China's forgetting jade . . . well, there are what you might call legends. And, like all legends, these are based on more than a little truth.

Recent travelers from China *say* that they have seen many Chinese, even Communist officials, pausing in their activities for a moment's reflection, reaching into their pockets to extract a piece of stone, which they caress between their fingers thoughtfully.

And, *it is said,* that even today in some Chinese households very special parties are still held, as they have been for hundreds of years. At these intimate gatherings no conversation is expected of the guests; instead, each brings a beloved piece of exquisitely carved jade, which is passed around among those assembled. With eyes closed, the mind at rest, each touches the jade with sensitive fingers and lets the thoughts wander as they will.

Legends? Perhaps. Or maybe the ageless beginning of another chapter in the story of jade.

BIBLIOGRAPHY

In addition to the hundreds of periodicals consulted, the author found the following books helpful:

Archaic Chinese Jades; special exhibition, February 1940. Philadelphia: University Museum.

Arden Gallery. *3000 years of Chinese Jade.* New York: 1939.

ASHTON, LEIGH, and GRAY, BASIL. *Chinese Art.* New York: Beechhurst Press, 1953.

Pre-Columbian Art: Robert Woods Bliss Collection. London: Phaidon Press, 1957.

COVARRUBIAS, MIGUEL. *Indian Art of Mexico and Central America.* New York: Alfred A. Knopf, 1957.

CREEL, HERRLEE GLESSNER. *The Birth of China.* New York: Ungar, 1937.

———. *Chinese Thought from Confucius to Mao Tse-tung.* Chicago: University of Chicago, 1953.

DEBARY, WM. THEODORE. *Sources of Chinese Tradition.* New York: Columbia University Press, 1960.

FEDDERSEN, MARTIN. *Chinese Decorative Art.* New York: Thomas Yoseloff, 1961.

FERGUSON, JOHN C. *Survey of Chinese Art.* Shanghai: Commercial Press, Ltd., 1939.

GOETTE, JOHN. *Jade Lore.* Shanghai: Kelly and Walsh, Ltd., 1936.

GROUSSET, RENE. *Chinese Art and Culture.* New York: Orion Press, 1959.

HANSFORD, S. HOWARD. *Chinese Jade Carving.* London: Lund Humphries & Co., 1950.

———. *Glossary of Chinese Art and Archeology.* London: The China Society, 1954.

I Ching, or Book of Changes. New York: Pantheon Press, 1953.

Investigations and Studies in Jade, the Heber R. Bishop collection. New York: Privately printed, 1906.

LATOURETTE, KENNETH SCOTT. *The Chinese Their History and Culture.* New York: Macmillan, 1953.

LEE, BOLTON. *What One Should Know About Jade.* Hong Kong: The Moon Gate, 1960.

LOO, C. T. An Exhibition of Chinese Archaic Jades . . . arranged for the Norton Gallery of Art, West Palm Beach, Florida, January 20 to March 1, 1950.

LAUFER, BERTHOLD. *Jade, A Study in Chinese Archeology and Religion.* Chicago: Field Museum of Natural History, 1912.

Pages of History. Jade in California. Sausalito, California: Pages of History, 1960.

PERRY, LILLA S. *Chinese Snuff Bottles.* Rutland, Vermont, and Tokyo, Japan: Charles E. Tuttle, 1960.

POPE-HENNESSEY, UNA. *A Jade Miscellany.* London: Nicholson and Watson, 1946.

——. *Early Chinese Jades.* London: Ernest Benn, Ltd., 1923.

SALMONY, ALFRED. *Carved Jade of Ancient China.* Berkeley, California: Gillick Press, 1938.

WALEY, ARTHUR. *The Book of Songs.* New York: Grove Press, 1960.

——. *Translations from the Chinese.* New York: Alfred A. Knopf, 1941.

Jades of the T. B. Walker collection at the Walker Art Center. Minneapolis, Minnesota.

WHITLOCK, HERBERT P., and EHRMANN, MARTIN L. *The Story of Jade.* New York: Sheridan House, 1949.

WILLIAMS, C. A. S. *Encyclopedia of Chinese Symbolism and Art Motives.* New York: The Julian Press, 1960.

WILSON, CAROL GREEN. *Gump's Treasure Trade.* New York: Thomas Y. Crowell, 1949.

AMERICAN MUSEUMS WITH NOTABLE JADE COLLECTIONS

M. H. De Young Memorial Museum, San Francisco, California (Avery Brundage collection)

The Seattle Art Museum, Seattle, Washington (Richard E. Fuller collection)

The Denver Art Museum, Denver, Colorado

The Art Institute of Chicago, Chicago, Illinois (Mr. and Mrs. Edward Sonnenschein collection)

Chicago Natural History Museum, Chicago, Illinois

Lizzadro Museum of Lapidary Arts, Elmhurst, Illinois

The Minneapolis Institute of Arts, Minneapolis, Minnesota (Alfred F. Pillsbury collection)

Walker Art Center, Minneapolis, Minnesota (T. B. Walker collection)

Dayton Art Center, Dayton, Ohio

The Metropolitan Museum of Art, New York, (Heber R. Bishop collection)

Brooklyn Museum, Brooklyn, New York

Fogg Art Museum, Harvard University, Cambridge, Massachusetts (Grenville L. Winthrop collection)

Natural History Museum, Smithsonian Institution, Washington, D.C. (Maude Monell Vetlesen collection)

National Gallery of Art, Washington, D.C. (Robert Woods Bliss collection)

The Freer Gallery of Art, Washington, D.C.

The William Rockhill Nelson Gallery of Art, Kansas City, Missouri

ACKNOWLEDGMENTS

The author gratefully acknowledges the expert help and advice of the following: Martin Rosenblatt, for the use of his extensive knowledge, appreciation, and library; Curt Gentry, for his editorial and research assistance; John Wenti Chang, Joseph Wheeler, John LaPlant, and K. Y. Ma, for their aid in deciphering some of the mysteries of jade; Zoray Andrus, for the art work in this volume; and Avery Brundage, whose famed art collection, a gift to the people of San Francisco, provided much of the material for this book.

Grateful acknowledgment is also made to the following individuals and museums for their help in obtaining information and/or illustrations: Jack V. Sewell, The Art Institute of Chicago; Kenneth Starr, Chicago Natural History Museum; Carl J. Weinhardt, Jr., Mrs. Edward H. Sirich, and Miss Inez M. Quinn, Minneapolis Institute of Arts; Martin Friedman, Walker Art Center; Alan Priest, Metropolitan Museum of Art; John Latham, Brooklyn Museum; Usher P. Coolidge, Fogg Art Museum; George Switzer, Smithsonian Institution; John Walker, Hereward Lester Cooke, National Gallery of Art; Archibald G. Wenley, the Freer Gallery of Art; Laurence Sickman, Miss Jeanne Harris, William Rockhill Nelson Gallery of Art; and Richard E. Fuller, Seattle Art Museum.

Acknowledgment is also made to the following publishers and authors who have graciously granted permission to quote from the books indicated: John Day, Pearl Buck, *My Several Worlds,* and Arnold Genthe, *I Remember;* Gillick Press, Alfred Salmony, *Carved Jade of Ancient China;* Grove Press, Arthur Waley, *The Book of Songs;* Kelly and Walsh, Ltd., John Goette, *Jade Lore;* Alfred A. Knopf, Miguel Covarrubias, *Indian Art of Mexico and Central America;* Lund Humphries & Co., S. Howard Hansford, *Chinese Jade Carving;* and Ungar, Herrlee Glessner Creel, *The Birth of China.*

INDEX